SWEET SEPTEMBER

Home to Heather Creek

Before the Dawn

Sweet September

HOME TO HEATHER CREEK™

SWEET SEPTEMBER

Tricia Goyer

Guideposts

Published by Guideposts Books & Inspirational Media
100 Reserve Road, Suite E200
Danbury, CT 06810
Guideposts.org

Cover by Lookout Design, Inc.
Interior design by Cindy LaBreacht
Additional design work by Müllerhaus
Typeset by Aptara, Inc.
Printed in the United States of America
10 9 8 7 6 5 4 3 2 1

Acknowledgments

To Nathan, my son. The adventures you dream up are almost as big as your caring heart. May both grow as you do. Books about people who love are only possible when one has received love grandly. Thanks go to the following: John, Cory, Leslie, Nathan, Grandma—the home team; Easthaven Baptist Church and Monday Night Small Group —the spiritual support; Janet—the best adviser ever; Carolyne, Leslie, Bob, Kristen—the writing squad; Beth— the squad captain; Jesus—my everything. Thank you! Thank you! Thank you!

—Tricia Goyer

Chapter One

The nip from the air seeping in through the cracked kitchen window caused a shiver to dance up Charlotte's spine. Autumn had slipped into summer's place without her realizing it.

Changes. More changes. It's all her life had been about lately.

The *beep-beep-beep* of the gaming device in Christopher's hands joined with the sound of bacon frying and the energetic tune from the radio in Emily's room. Charlotte imagined Emily using the curling iron to curl her straight blonde hair, just as she herself had used an iron to straighten her curls when she was fourteen.

"Two pieces of bacon, Christopher?" Charlotte asked the ten-year-old.

"Yes, please."

She noted the edges of his lips curl into a smile though he neither looked up from his game nor gave any hint that he'd noticed the plate in front of him stacked with his favorite chocolate chip pancakes. Lightning, Christopher's cat, weaved around the boy's feet, but even he couldn't distract his owner this morning.

Charlotte turned off the burner and carried the plate of bacon to the table, using the tongs to place two pieces on Christopher's plate.

From across the table, Bob took a sip of his coffee and then sniffed the air. "I'll have what he's having." He reached for a slice of bacon, and Charlotte swatted his hand.

"You know what you *really* want is to finish that oatmeal, mister, and then get cleaned up. I have some errands in town today I was hoping you could help with."

Without a word, Bob pursed his lips, picked up his spoon, and unenthusiastically scooped up a spoonful of the steaming porridge. Changing his eating habits due to his diabetes hadn't been easy on him. He stared at the oatmeal as if it were glue, even turning the spoon upside down to watch it plop back into the bowl.

Wiping her hands on her apron, Charlotte moved past the pantry, down the hallway to the stairs, and then jogged up them toward the bathroom. As she did, she was certain she heard the sound of his fork scooping up a slice of bacon.

"I may have gray in my hair, but that doesn't mean my hearing's gone yet," she called over her shoulder, loud enough for Bob to hear.

"What did you say?" he called back. But she knew full well he'd heard. Instead of bantering with her husband, she knocked on the bathroom door.

"Breakfast."

The gurgle from the water in the bathroom sink shut off and the door swung open. Sam offered no smile, and instead tossed his dark hair, once then twice, glancing in the mirror to make sure it laid *just so* across his forehead.

Towering over her, Sam peered over Charlotte's head and down the stairs, cocking his head.

"That's the music from Mario . . . is Christopher playing a game? I thought he was supposed to be studying for his spelling test?" He raised his voice.

"It *is* a game. I'm surprised you can hear that." Charlotte cocked an eyebrow. "Um-hum. Now I know you can hear me when I call you down for chores." Charlotte placed a hand on her grandson's arm. "But don't you worry about Christopher's spelling. We already took care of it this morning. He got them all right, two times in a row."

"Sorry, Grams." Sam offered an apologetic smile. "It's just that one of us Slaters needs to make the honor roll, and I vote for Christopher."

She pursed her lips and nodded. Even though Sam smirked at his joke, Charlotte could see more in his gaze. Once again, she was amazed at Sam's fierce care for his brother and sister. She reminded herself again that their lives hadn't hit the reset button the moment they'd arrived on her doorstep. They'd already had a lot of heartache in their young lives—first with their father's abandonment, heading off to places unknown. And now their mother's death. *Please, Lord, help me remember to make it easier—not harder—for the kids to adjust and help me to not take it personally. Let Sam learn to trust us to care for Emily and Christopher. And for him too—though Sam doesn't like to admit he needs caring for.*

"And what about you?" she asked as Sam squeezed through the doorway past her. "Didn't see any books come out of your backpack last night."

Sam shrugged. She followed him down the stairs. He entered the kitchen and turned his chair backward, straddling it. Then, in one motion, he filled his plate with pancakes and bacon. "Don't know. Maybe the teachers decided to go easy on us for a change." Sam popped a piece of bacon in his mouth and wiped his greasy fingers on his pants.

Charlotte lifted one eyebrow but said nothing. *They're only pants*, she reminded herself. *Besides, it seems like the more ripped up and stained, the more kids like them these days.*

Lightning wove his thin body around the legs of the dining room chairs, keeping his eye on the table for any sign of a nibble cast his direction.

The cat meowed once, and Sam pushed him aside gently with his sock-covered foot. Christopher didn't look up from his game.

"Where did you get that thing anyway, Chris? Let me see it." Sam held out his hand.

"Uncle Pete picked it up at a yard sale in town," Charlotte answered, striding up to the table. "Says it's as old as you are, but Christopher doesn't seem to mind."

"Give it." Sam glared at his brother.

Christopher frowned but passed the electronic game to Sam, who eagerly picked up where Christopher left off.

"Grandma, can I take a walk?" Christopher asked. "I still got time before the bus arrives."

"Sure." Charlotte rubbed her hand over his close-cropped blond hair. "But don't get too far, hear? I don't want to lose my voice having to call after you. I have to holler enough around here, keeping your Uncle Pete out of trouble."

Christopher cleared his plate, tossing his napkin in the

trash. No sooner did he exit the back door than she heard Pete's heavy footsteps stomping as he wiped his boots on the mat. She also heard Christopher repeating their conversation. The door swung open with a loud bang as it hit the wall, and Pete entered with an over-exaggerated scowl.

"I hear someone in here is calling me *Trouble*," he said in the same loud voice he used to call to his friends across the parking lot of the feed store.

"No, I said I'm keeping someone *out of trouble*. There's a difference, you know."

Pete shrugged but didn't say a word as he occupied the seat Christopher had just emptied. A smile filled his face as he saw Sam intent on the game in his hands. Soon two sets of eyes were fixed on the small screen.

"Grandma?" It was Emily's voice from the top of the stairs.

"Hmm?" Charlotte answered, getting herself a piece of bacon from the plate and nibbling on one end.

"Do you think you can make me a smoothie? My nails are wet, and I'm waiting for Ashley to call me back. She's checking to see if she can stay over tonight. It's something called teacher in-service and there's no school. You said it was all right, didn't you?"

"Yes, and yes. One monkey-berry, coming up." Charlotte tore off a banana from the bunch and placed it by the small green carton of strawberries on the counter. Then she pulled the blender from the cupboard. She was glad Emily and Ashley were becoming so close. Emily still texted her friends from San Diego sometimes, but she wasn't as obsessed with her cell phone as she had been when the kids had first come to the farm in the spring. Sam hadn't even bothered to get a new charger for his phone and didn't seem to mind that it didn't work.

"With yogurt too—" Emily's words were cut off by the phone ringing.

"With yogurt too." Charlotte nodded, knowing she was talking to thin air at the top of the stairs. She could hear Emily answering it on the upstairs extension in the guest room.

"You shouldn't be catering to the girl." Bob rose and took his dirty jean jacket off the back of the chair, sliding it on as he stood. "You know it's not healthy for her—"

"It is healthy," Charlotte interrupted. "It's fruit, yogurt, and milk. Everything Emily eats is healthy."

"But kids need protein for strong muscles. How in the world is she going to have energy for her chores? Harvest starts tomorrow and these kids aren't going to know what hit them."

It was obvious Sam didn't see the humor. He set down the game and let out a groan. "More work?"

Charlotte ignored her grandson, keeping her eyes fixed on her husband. Then Charlotte lowered her voice. "So the girl doesn't like meat. That's why I always add an extra ingredient." She tossed two scoops of protein powder into the blender, then winked at Bob. "In fact, maybe we all should follow her lead. It wouldn't hurt us the slightest."

Bob approached. She reached out a hand and patted his round paunch, which hung over his belt buckle.

"*Humph.*" The grunt was both a sign of Bob's disapproval and his good-bye. He placed a kiss on her cheek and headed out the back door like he'd done every day of their married life. She watched him from the kitchen window. One would think by his quickened pace that he still ran the farm without any help. In truth, Pete had already taken care of the morning chores.

Charlotte noted Pete's gaze also following his father's footsteps. "Don't know why he does that," Pete grumbled, returning his attention to his plate. "Does he still think he needs to check up on everything I do? It's not like I'm a kid anymore. But you watch, Dad's gonna come back in with some comment—something I missed."

Charlotte waved a hand his direction. "Nonsense. He's just trying to feel needed, that's all. You know he doesn't like being unable to do what he used to. You realize, don't you, that years from now when our Maker calls him home, he's going to be arguing that he can't leave until the cows are in?"

"Not like arguing makes any difference." Sam rose and tossed his dark hair, like the skater boys he liked to watch on TV. "Arguing doesn't make one difference when it comes to your time to go . . . or about chores."

Sam set down his plate in the sink and then he rubbed his hands together like a little kid in a candy store.

"Harvest, hmm? Wee-ha! Can't wait." Sam faked eagerness. "Fun, fun, fun."

Chapter Two

Christopher sniffed the air as he headed across the field, wondering how far he could make it before his grandma called him back. Toby barked at him from the porch. He wished he could stay home all day instead of having to ride in the noisy bus or sit in class and practice fractions. He hated fractions.

The air smelled kind of like those scented crayons his mom used to buy for him on his birthday. The brown crayon smelled like the air did today. In the fields, everything had turned from bright green to dark green, and now to golden brown. Christopher wondered, though, how they got the smell of earth into that brown crayon. Maybe he'd have to find a book that would tell him. Or ask his teacher. She seemed to know everything.

From somewhere in the field, a bird called out to Christopher, and he decided to veer off the well-worn path to the creek. He glanced over his shoulder and noticed the white house was still within calling distance. That was the term he'd come up with after he'd figured out what was too far according to Grandma. Or, more accurately, Grandma's voice.

He hadn't taken more than ten steps when something caught his eye on the ground near a tall oak tree. He spotted it just seconds before it caught on the toe of his shoe. He nearly tripped, then smiled as he caught himself. At least he wouldn't have to explain how his school clothes got so dirty so fast.

Christopher hunched down to take a closer look at the object and then pulled a small stick—not much longer than his hand—out of his back pocket. He'd found it was useful to carry a stick around to poke at things. It meant he didn't have to wash up as much, which was a good thing, in his opinion.

He poked at the metal object and the dirt around it, realizing it was bigger than the one corner that poked out of the ground. Then with the edge of the stick, he scraped away the moist dirt, faster and faster, his excitement building with his find.

The bird called again, and he knew that Grandma's voice would soon be calling too. He grabbed two sides of the piece of metal and rocked it back and forth until it came free with a sucking sound as he pulled it from the earth.

It was an oval contraption about the size and shape of a toy drum. It was brown and rusty, and it appeared to have been in the dirt longer than he was old. Maybe even older than Uncle Pete. Not thinking anymore about his school clothes or washing up, Christopher pressed it to his chest and hurried toward the house. But as he neared, he changed his mind.

He could almost hear his grandma's voice saying, "Get that dirty thing out of this house." Either that or she would just throw it out when he wasn't looking. Grandma, it seemed, didn't know good treasure when she saw it.

So instead of heading toward the back porch, Christopher veered off and hurried to the tractor shed. If he guessed right, he had enough time to hide his find, brush off his clothes, wash his hands, and *still* make the bus.

Chapter Three

Charlotte didn't realize she was holding her breath as her ears perked to the sounds of Emily's footsteps coming down the stairs. She let out the smallest sigh of relief as Emily emerged, wearing a serious expression, and also wearing the one pair of jeans that actually fit her and weren't skintight.

Without a word, Emily lifted the pink smoothie from the counter and took a long drink. The smallest pink moustache graced her top lip, but she quickly licked it away with the tip of her tongue.

"You look nice today. I like your hair like that."

Just like your mother used to wear it, Charlotte wanted to add but didn't—for both their sakes. Still, an ache filled her chest as she looked into her granddaughter's eyes, again praying a silent prayer that, as a grandma, she would do better on the child rearing this time around.

"Ashley *can* stay the night, and I was wondering if we could stay up and watch a movie. Maybe that funny one Uncle Pete let us borrow. Ashley hasn't seen it yet—"

Charlotte frowned, thinking about Pete's taste in movies. She'd definitely have to check to see if it was on the approved list.

Sam stood and grabbed a soccer ball off the floor, tossing it back and forth in his hands, with his long arms stretching from side to side to catch it. Months ago a ball being tossed around her dining room—and all her antiques displayed in the hutch—would have made Charlotte anxious. Now she was hardly fazed. She was just glad he wasn't kicking it.

"I wouldn't get your hopes up about a movie," Sam butted in. "I've already gotten the lecture that we should expect a lot of chores tomorrow." Then he mouthed the word *harvest*.

"He's kidding, right?" Emily cocked one eyebrow. "I'm still sore from all the stuff you made us do last weekend." She rubbed her thin arms for emphasis.

Charlotte heard the back door open and watched a blur of boy zip by as Christopher hurried around the corner, up the stairs, and into the bathroom.

"You're looking at this all wrong." Charlotte brushed a lock of hair behind her ear, making a mental note to schedule a haircut. "Harvest is my favorite time of year. It's a time to celebrate the good bounty the Lord has provided, and the fact that He's taken care of us for another year. Besides, it's the harvest that pays for that smoothie in your hand and the polish on those nails. There's nothing wrong with a little hard work."

She could tell by the look on Sam and Emily's faces they weren't buying her pep talk. She heard the water shut off in the bathroom sink and spotted Christopher emerging, shaking droplets of water from his hands. The rumble of the school bus approaching caused them all to turn to the window. And there was a second rumbling, just under Charlotte's ribcage, that told her Christopher was up to something.

"I like the harvest, Grandma," Christopher blurted out. He ran out the back door before she had a chance to remind him to dry his hands or to ask what he was up to.

Sam dropped the soccer ball, letting it bounce and roll to a stop in the corner, and grabbed his backpack, swinging it over his shoulder. "Come on, Betty Sue. We must hurry and catch the wagon to the one-room schoolhouse, or we'll have to walk to school, both ways, *uphill*."

"Coming. I only hope you remembered an apple for the teacher. I think she's really swell."

Both older kids nodded a good-bye before they headed out the door. Charlotte watched as they hurried to the school bus.

It was only a few weeks into the school year, but the kids had adjusted to their new schedules. Christopher liked his new teacher, Mrs. Wright, and Emily had moved up to the high school this year, which seemed to suit her just fine.

Charlotte watched as they climbed onto the bus and chose their seats. Sam sat close to the front because he couldn't be bothered to walk all the way to the back with the other teenagers. Emily sat in the middle next to a classmate Charlotte recognized but whose name she couldn't recall. Even from this distance, Charlotte could make out how the two girls turned toward each other, both of their mouths moving at once. And Christopher sat close enough to the back to get a sense that he was sitting with the big kids, but far enough away not to cause any trouble with them.

Charlotte waved as the bus drove away—though no one probably noticed. Then she turned to scan the now-empty kitchen.

Who was she fooling? It wasn't empty at all. Breakfast dishes were still stacked on the table. Clumps of mud rested on the floor where Pete had sat, despite the fact he'd stomped his boots by the back door. A trail of more mud followed the path to the bathroom where Christopher had scampered before heading off to school.

Charlotte made a mental note to check the bathroom vanity for one of Christopher's treasures. No doubt she'd find a special rock or bird's feather.

But first... Charlotte poured herself a cup of coffee and grabbed her Bible from its place on the hutch. Then she settled down in her favorite dining room chair, which provided a view out the window of her men hard at work—the two working side by side, yet not really together. Their own stubborn pride kept them from connecting as she'd always hoped they would.

But enough of those worries.

Charlotte opened her Bible to where she'd been reading in Ruth. It's a story she'd found herself returning to, a story of family bonds that tendered her heart. A story she always seemed to be drawn to at harvest. The thought of the young woman, dear Ruth, gleaning the fields was one she could relate to. Charlotte could almost picture the sweat on Ruth's brow as she followed the harvesters, gathering armfuls of provision for her and her mother-in-law, just doing what she had to after they'd lost so much. It was in her cheerful heart, and in being obedient to Naomi's request, that Ruth found favor in both Boaz's and God's eyes.

Although Charlotte didn't know if it was the right interpretation, lately she'd liked to imagine God looking upon her as Boaz looked at Ruth, gazing down with favor.

Charlotte glided her finger down the page and came to the passage in chapter two, verses eleven and twelve—the one she liked best. She felt the sun on her shoulders and smiled as she read the words to herself, imagining Boaz speaking them to Ruth:

"I have heard how you left your father and mother and your own land to live here among complete strangers. May the Lord, the God of Israel, under whose wings you have come to take refuge, reward you fully."

Charlotte closed the Bible and placed it on the scarred table on which hundreds of meals had been served over the years. And in her soul, she ate those words as hungrily as the men of the house had gobbled up their breakfast. The message fed her, strengthened her. And though the situation wasn't the same, she could relate.

She had been the one welcoming in the children, but she understood what it was like to feel like a stranger in a strange land. If parenting three young kids in this decade—and at her age—wasn't strange, she didn't know what was.

Charlotte also liked the idea of nestling under the Lord's wings. She'd gathered enough eggs in her day to fully appreciate the softness, warmth, and security found under them.

Finally, she clung to the idea that God was her refuge. Sure, she was surrounded by a flurry of activity, but it was moments like these where she found a safe haven, a shelter of rest. It was also in these quiet moments she gained the strength to create a haven of security for her grandchildren.

Charlotte closed her eyes and prayed a silent prayer for those she loved. *Lord, reward us fully, this day. Not with things of this world, for that we have no need. But with more of You, Lord. More of You.*

Chapter Four

Charlotte tried not to chuckle at the glassy-eyed looks the four children offered her the next morning. Though there was no school this Friday, Bob insisted they get up early. "Kids gotta know what real work is like," he'd insisted the previous night. And just because Ashley was a guest didn't give her a hall pass.

"Sorry you hafta do chores on our day off," Emily said to Ashley, taking a bite of the bran muffin placed before her.

Ashley shrugged, her red curls poking out from under a baseball cap that read *Cougars*. "No different at my house. There's always chores, even though we do live in town. Maybe together we can get them done sooner." The young girl wiped crumbs from her lip with her fingers and then glanced up at Charlotte. "Are we gonna take out the pipes?"

"Pipes?" It was the first word Sam spoke all morning.

Charlotte set her coffee mug on the oak table and nodded. "Irrigation pipes. You know the ones we laid out. The ones whose gates you've been changing for water flow to the fields. They have to be removed before Uncle Pete gets the combine out."

"Yeah, I know. But there are a lot of them. That'll be a lot of work."

From across the table, Bob glanced up from his open Bible and scowled. She didn't know if it was because they were talking too much during his traditional quiet time or because she mentioned it would be Pete who would be running the combine this year.

"It shouldn't take too long," Charlotte added, tapping Christopher's shoulder and pointing to his plate. Instead of looking at her, he stared at the bran muffin as if she'd just placed a clump of manure on his plate. "Uncle Pete got most of the pipe up while you were at school, but . . ."

Her words were interrupted as Christopher sucked in a dramatic breath, pinched his nose, and took a bite of the muffin. He closed his eyes and chewed with extra emphasis, no doubt knowing all eyes were on him. After a few more chews his eyes popped open. "Not bad." He unpinched his nose and took another bite. Then he dropped a crumb to the floor. Lightning quickly licked it up. "See," Christopher added, "even Lightning likes it!"

Charlotte chuckled. "I'm glad you and Lightning approve."

She turned back to the girls. "As I was saying, if we work hard today—and tomorrow morning—maybe we can all go to town Saturday afternoon."

Emily cocked an eyebrow, and Charlotte imagined her thoughts: *As if there is anything to do in town.*

Ashley jumped to her feet. "Great. C'mon." She tugged

at Emily's arm. Christopher finished his muffin, scrambled eggs and turkey sausage, and then dropped to the floor and quickly put on his shoes.

He patted Lightning once and then jumped to his feet. "I'm going . . . outside," he spouted, and Charlotte didn't miss the mischievous twinkle in his eyes that could only mean one thing. Christopher had most likely found another "treasure" he was keeping under wraps. Since she hadn't seen anything in the bathroom yesterday, she knew it had to be something big—something worth hiding.

"So if I do this will I be eligible for 4-H?" Sam smirked.

Bob opened his mouth, and Charlotte reached for the coffeepot before he had a chance to speak.

"Need a refill, hon?" She poured him a second cup without waiting for an answer.

He glanced at her and closed his mouth again. She could see his mind replaying the scene and coming up with a better response.

"You kiddin'? Four-H, why that's just the start," Bob finally said. "There's nothin' like starting up a combine and driving it through the fields—knowing that because of your hard work, your family will be warm and well-fed all winter."

"I'd rather be driving a convertible to the beach." Sam rose and slipped on one of Pete's old work jackets. "At least that would make having my learner's permit worthwhile."

At least he's doing what he's told, Charlotte thought. *We'll work on obedience first . . . and attitude later.*

"You kiddin'?" Bob said for the second time in one minute. "I'm not going to drive a car that isn't even decent enough to keep out the rain."

"Yeah, well, that's because in San Diego we don't have—"

"Grandma, Grandma!" Christopher rushed in the door, interrupting his brother. "Come quick."

Charlotte jumped to her feet. "Something wrong? Someone get hurt?"

"Yeah . . . the garden. It's all tore up!"

CHARLOTTE'S FIRST THOUGHT as she looked out at the garden was that during the night the farm animals decided to have a square dance in the middle of her peas and carrots. She walked forward, her feet sinking into the soft dirt, to get a closer look.

"Look, Grandma." Christopher raced forward, pointing to the rows. "That's where the carrots were for my cake. 'Member I was gonna pick them and you said to wait until Sunday then we could bake it together. And the yellow squash . . ." He raced over and pointed to the far row. "The three small ones are gone!"

"Stop, Christopher. Get back here. Look what you're doing!" Sam ambled over. Even the news that the garden was uprooted hadn't caused him to move any faster then necessary. "You've gone and done it now. You've ruined all the evidence."

"Evidence for what?" Emily and Ashley approached, each one carrying a barn cat that had no desire to be held. The cats twisted and turned, attempting to break free, but to no avail.

"Evidence of the thief—it has to be a two-legged kind. I can't imagine a rabbit or deer carrying off squash." He pointed to the row. "But look. You've trampled over every-thing. There's no way we can look for footprints now."

While the kids argued, Charlotte crossed her arms over her chest, a sinking feeling coming over her. Whether it was animals or even a person, she'd planned on that pro-duce. Three extra mouths to feed hadn't been good on the budget. The warm Indian summer had helped the garden flourish even later than usual. And now this.

"Why don't we let Uncle Pete look at it and come to a conclusion? He'll know—"

She heard the sound of someone clearing his throat and noticed Bob standing there. His eyes weren't on the garden, but on her. He had an angry look as if she'd just slapped him in the face.

"It's animals—that's for sure. People around here don't do that to each other. It's not California. But what's done is done . . . ain't nothing we can do about it now. So I'd sug-gest everyone stop their gawking and get to work."

Charlotte nodded, but inside she was unsure what she'd said to get Bob in such a huff. It wasn't like she was doing anything wrong. In fact, she went out of her way to try to foster peace between all members of their new family unit. What felt like a rock settled in the pit of her stomach and a new wave of weariness washed over her.

"Do as your grandpa says, kids. Load up in the truck, and he'll show you what to do." She forced a smile and patted Christopher's shoulder. "We'll talk more about this mystery at lunch."

Charlotte watched as the kids hurried over to the truck. She tucked her hands in her pockets as the girls climbed in the cab. Sam jumped onto the flatbed and reached down to help Christopher up. She opened her mouth to call a reminder to Sam to make sure Christopher didn't get too wild, especially around the farm equipment, but changed her mind. Sam did watch out for Christopher. He didn't need her nagging and reminding him all the time. She waved as she watched the truck rumble out to the far soybean field, remembering how Denise always complained that Charlotte was "on her" all the time and didn't give her room to breathe. Those words had haunted her when her daughter first ran away at age eighteen, and they'd been resurrected, replaying every time she thought about reprimanding the kids . . . reminding them, or as Denise would say, nagging them.

She turned and crossed her arms over her chest, taking in the sight of her garden. Whoever . . . whatever . . . sure had a field day. She sighed, leaning over to pluck up a carrot top devoid of carrot. *One more thing to think about. Something else to clean up.*

Quick footsteps led her to the tool shed to retrieve a hoe. "No time like the present to complete a distasteful task," Charlotte mumbled to herself, repeating one of her mother's favorite phrases. She lifted the hoe, the wood of the handle scratching her palm, and her ears perked to the sound of a car coming up the driveway. She tilted her head to listen closer. It was definitely a car. It didn't have the deep rumble of Bob's truck or the sputtering sound from Pete's rig that he'd named *Lazarus*—due to the fact it had been resurrected more times than they could count.

She returned the hoe, wiped her hand on her jeans, and

hurried toward the car. It was a small red compact car—one she didn't recognize from around town. The Indian summer sun gleamed on the window, and through the glare she barely made out someone inside waving. Charlotte shielded her eyes and walked from the doorway of the barn toward the driveway.

Before she reached it, the car parked and a young woman slid out of the front seat. She was tall with straight dark hair that brushed her shoulders. She smiled and waved, then glanced around as if expecting to see someone else.

"Hello, uh, Mrs. Stevenson. Do you remember me?"

Charlotte cocked her head, taking in her round face, the bangs fringed on her forehead and the slightest crinkles at the corners of her eyes when she smiled.

The woman laughed. "Okay, maybe this will help." She took her bangs and lifted them straight. "Just imagine me with big hair and bright makeup."

"Dana?" Charlotte rushed forward. "Why, I haven't seen you since . . ."

"Since the early nineties when I headed to college. I know. It's been so long, which just blows my mind because . . . well." She glanced around. "You know." She shrugged. "I spent so much time here."

Charlotte closed the gap and grasped her hands. "And I loved every minute of it, especially after Den—" The word wouldn't come. Charlotte felt as if an apple core was stuck in her throat. She covered her mouth with her hand. "I'm sorry. It should be easier by now."

Dana squeezed her hands. "I understand. And I'm sorry

I didn't contact you sooner. I just moved back into town. But once I found out . . . Hold on—" She released Charlotte's hands and moved to her car, pulling a small vase filled with roses from the passenger's seat. She approached and offered her gift. "I brought these. They are the last blooms from Grandma's garden. She insisted I bring them over. She doesn't get out much and can't hear well on the phone. Otherwise she would have called you sooner to offer her sympathy."

Charlotte took in the sight of the young woman, remembering how many hopes she'd wrapped around her. Dana had dated Pete for most of their high school years. Every prom photo and snapshot of Pete in high school had Dana in it. They were best friends as well as being romantically involved.

She took the vase from the young woman, noticing no ring on her finger.

Charlotte smiled and breathed in the scent. "Well, you thank her for me, will you? And please come inside . . . it's a mess with the kids and all, but I made some muffins this morning. They must be half-decent because the kids ate most of them."

Dana glanced at her watch. "I have about thirty minutes before I head back to school. The kids get the day off, but not me."

Charlotte took a few steps before realizing Dana didn't follow. She glanced back over her shoulder.

"And, well, there's another reason for my visit too . . . it's not as pleasant." Dana tapped her lower lip with her pointer finger.

"Is something wrong?" Suddenly the heavy scent of roses overwhelmed her.

"I'm back this year, as a teacher. I'm Miss Simons, Sam's third-period English teacher." She pulled a piece of paper out of her back pocket and stretched it out to Charlotte. "It's Sam's essay. He, uh, turned it in this way—all folded up."

Charlotte balanced the vase against her hip and took the paper from Dana's hand. "I had heard Sam mention a Miss Simons but I never made the connection. I suppose I need to read it?"

Dana nodded. "Yeah." She offered a smile. "But I'm game for a muffin if you're still offering. I'll pour the coffee, if you have any left from breakfast."

Dana led the way, and Charlotte followed, slowly unfolding the paper, shaking it out with one hand. The paper only held seven words. "Life stinks. Nebraska stinks. End of essay."

CHARLOTTE SIPPED her warmed-up coffee and watched as the sweet high schooler from her memory transformed into a serious teacher before her eyes.

"You know, I really prayed about how I should handle this." Dana's hands spread over the paper, as if trying to iron out the wrinkles. "I'm a tough teacher. I want the kids to respect me. But more than that, I want to prepare them for the real world. It was a shocker going off to college. I went from feeling like I was at the top of my class to worrying if I'd pass. Mrs. Anthony was great ... don't get me wrong. But, well, in college you can't talk your way into a better grade by bringing in a couple of jars of Grandma's homemade applesauce."

"I understand that you need to give him the grade he deserves." Though as Charlotte said the words, she had a sinking feeling . . . *Sam did just lose his mom . . . and moved to a new world.* But, then again, he'd also been spending a lot of time on other things—on everything else around the farm—rather than on his studies. And, too often, Sam spent more time with Pete than she thought he should.

"Well, I've come to a compromise," Dana said. "Sam will get a second chance, but he has to do twice as much work. And I want it by the end of the month. What first was a two-page essay will now be a four-page report on Nebraska. The good things about this state."

Charlotte noticed Dana said "this" state, instead of "our" state. She had a million questions about why Dana had decided to go to college in Chicago in the first place, what had happened between her and Pete, and what had kept her away so long. Yet Charlotte had to remind herself this wasn't the good ol' days. This was a different day. Dana —or Miss Simons—was now Sam's teacher.

She pushed the plate of muffins closer to the younger woman. "That sounds like a good compromise to me. He should be grateful to have a second chance."

"Yes, well . . . it's the least I could do, considering all that he's been through recently."

Charlotte sat contentedly with Dana, pulling apart her muffin and placing the small pieces into her mouth. They made small talk about the growth of the town—two new gas stations in the last ten years—and the recent blue-ribbon winners at the county fair. Charlotte couldn't help but notice the woman's attention turning to the window over Charlotte's shoulder. When the conversation lagged once again, Charlotte decided to get everything out in the open.

"Pete is out in the field with the kids and Bob. They're gathering up pipe—getting ready for the soybean harvest."

"It's that time of year, isn't it? I did see Bill at the post office a few weeks ago. He said everyone is about the same as always."

Charlotte noted questions in the woman's gaze. "Pete's pretty much the same. Same old guy—happiest getting dirty out in the fields."

Dana glanced down. "Maybe I'll run into him in town one of these days."

"Or maybe I can invite Sam's teacher over for dinner sometime?"

"Actually, I prefer that you don't." Dana rose and carried her empty coffee cup to the sink. "It's probably better for Sam if . . . well, I don't want my past to complicate things." Dana took her car keys from her front jean pocket.

Charlotte wanted to insist that it would be nothing more than a home-cooked meal with an old friend, but in the end decided the young woman—Miss Simons—was right. Sam's grades were enough to focus on for the time being.

She slipped the piece of paper, Sam's essay, into the back pocket of her jeans.

More than enough.

Chapter Five

Laughter filled the air, and Charlotte lifted her head, turning her attention away from the garden toward the group hurrying from behind the large red barn where Bob had parked the truck. Everyone seemed to be talking at once. Charlotte couldn't make it out.

She figured it out when Bob rounded the corner of the barn, wet from head to toe. His gray-brown hair lay limp on his forehead, yet the slightest grin played on his lips.

Charlotte lifted her hands. "Hold it, hold it. I want to hear *this* story."

Christopher piped up before the others. "Grandpa and Sam made a bet."

"Yes, they raced to see who could stack the most pipe." Emily giggled. "And the loser had to wade into Heather Creek and then squat down so the water was over his head."

"Squat?" Charlotte placed her hands on her hips. She wagged her head at her husband. "You're not the young buck you used to be. What if you had gotten a catch in your knee while you were down there?"

"I don't think he took the time to worry about that. He was in the water and out again in ten seconds." Pete added.

"Mom, you should have seen it. I've never seen Dad move that fast."

"He was like the Road Runner on those old cartoons." Christopher laughed and hurried toward the house. "I'll draw you a picture of what it looked like."

The other kids also hurried inside, and Charlotte was sure their first stop would be the fridge. She glanced at Bob and lifted an eyebrow.

With the kids out of sight he placed both hands on his lower back and stretched. "Well, it worked. You should have seen those kids hustle. Only problem is I think I chilled myself to the bone. Maybe my bride can give me a back rub tonight?" Bob's eyes twinkled in a way they hadn't since Denise's accident.

Rolling his eyes, Pete started back toward the barn. "People, please."

"Yes, well, we'll have to see about that. In the meantime I think you should know we had a special visitor to Heather Creek Farm today—a Miss Dana Simons." Charlotte raised her voice, emphasizing the last three words.

Pete stopped midstep and turned. His face displayed both curiosity and fear. He hurried toward her, brushing his brown hair from his forehead.

"And what did you tell her . . . that I was still here on the farm?" His words stopped short. Red tinged his cheeks, and he looked away.

"Dana? I haven't seen her for ages." Bob placed an arm around Charlotte's shoulders. "I hope you invited her back for dinner."

"No, because I'm afraid she came to talk about Sam. It

seems she's his English teacher and he . . . well, there are a few struggles . . . you know, with so much going on."

Thankfully Bob didn't probe for details. He was too busy studying his son's face.

Pete removed his green John Deere cap and scratched the top of his head. Though he didn't say a word, Charlotte spotted what she thought to be a hint of interest and something else too. Embarrassment maybe. After all, Dana had left Bedford, lived other places, and experienced new things while Pete was still on the farm, just where she'd left him.

The front door opened, and Sam sauntered outside, his hands tucked deep in his pockets. "Hey, Grandma . . . is there any more pizza left over from the other day?"

"Sam . . . that was three days ago," she called back. "What do you think the answer is?"

He turned back to go into the house, but Pete hurried forward. "Hey, buddy, I have to head into town to pick up some things from the feed store. How about you come with me and we'll stop by Rosa's Pizza on the way home?"

A smile spread on Sam's face, and Charlotte knew pizza was only part of it. She saw the way Sam often watched Pete with interest—and awe. Perhaps it was due to the fact that Sam hadn't been reared with a male role model. Or maybe because they were similar in more ways than one.

"Whatever it takes to motivate a guy . . . or two." Bob chuckled. He turned to the garden, taking it in. "So—"

His words were interrupted as the girls darted through the back door, down the steps and hurried toward Charlotte.

"Grandma, we have a great idea." Emily had a smudge

of dirt on her nose, and Charlotte resisted the urge to wipe it away.

"Since Ashley was so much help today, I was thinking she should stay the night again. She said she's helped with a soybean harvest before on her grandparents' farm."

"My grandpa was teaching me to drive the grain truck."

"Well, this grandpa most likely won't let that happen . . ." Bob scoffed.

"But I think it's a great idea." Bob's eyebrows shot up, and Charlotte patted his arm. "The spending the night, not the driving." She tucked a strand of Emily's light hair behind her ear. She tried to do the same with Ashley's hair, but the red curl just bounced back in place. "If it's okay with Ashley's mom, that is."

She saw Christopher scurry across the yard toward the barn.

"In the meantime," Charlotte said. "I need to check on your brother. He's up to something . . . he's had a mischievous air about him lately."

⌣ Chapter
Six

Christopher hurried past the barn to the tractor shed behind it. He opened the door just wide enough to light up the inside. His eyes darted around, looking for spiders before he walked in. He hated spiders.

He dropped to his knees and pulled his treasure from behind the big, yellow bucket. Christopher turned the metal thing over in his hands, studying its shape and size. Last night, when he was trying to fall asleep, his mind kept going faster than the speed of light, figuring out what it could be. Maybe it was an Indian pot for cooking. The only problem was he couldn't figure out how to get the food inside of it. Or even worse, out of it when it was done.

But as he lay there in his bed in the dark and heard the sound of something moving outside, he finally figured out what it was. It had to be a part of an old spaceship, and whoever lost it long ago had realized it was now found. An alien? They'd be good aliens, of course, 'cause, so far from what he'd seen of Nebraska, everyone was nice.

He stuck it back behind the bucket when he heard his grandma's voice calling him. He brushed off his pants and yawned. He was tired—that was for sure—but maybe if the aliens came back tonight he could meet them. He was almost sure they were the ones who got into the garden. And maybe they'd have some idea where his dad is. After all, they could see the whole earth from outer space.

Christopher grinned, imagining how happy Sam would be about that.

He snuck back out of the shed and hurried to find his grandma before she got too worried. She worried a lot. Even though she never said so, he could see it in her eyes— just like how Mom had worried sometimes. In fact there were days when Grandma looked at him and it seemed like she was Mom, since their look was so much the same.

"Grandma!" He hurried away from the shed and toward her. He wrapped his arms around her. He smiled as she played with his hair, just like Mom used to do too.

"You wanna take a walk to the creek and show me the spot where Grandpa jumped in?"

"Can I bring the fishing pole Uncle Pete got me?"

"Let me guess: Did he get that at the yard sale?

Christopher shrugged. "Guess so."

"Sure, I might even show you how to cast."

"You know how to fish, Grandma?" He imagined her sitting in a boat and bringing in a big one like they did on those TV shows Uncle Pete liked to watch.

"Sure, I know a lot about fishing. The bigger the better." She reached down and wrapped one arm around his shoulder, and then tickled him with her free hand. "And then they flop, and they flop, and they flop," she said. Her fingers found the spot right in his armpit. How did she know where it tickled?

Fact was, even if he caught a fish, there was no way he would cook it or especially eat it. But he didn't need to tell Grandma that. He'd keep it a secret.

Christopher finally pulled away, sucked in a huge breath, and glanced back at the shed. It was just one secret . . . along with a few others.

Chapter
Seven

Dinner was finished, the kitchen clean, and the girls had already headed upstairs with plans to give each other makeovers. Charlotte sat on the sofa and separated colored embroidery threads into neat rows on the coffee table in front of her. She could hear Christopher playing in the bathtub upstairs with his plastic dinosaurs. Some type of battle was ensuing between the T. rexes and the three-horns—or so Christopher called them—and she wasn't looking forward to the sight of the bathroom floor when he was done. No doubt more water would be out of the tub than in it.

She was sure Christopher never would confess to still playing with toys in the tub. He'd most likely deny it. It was only the battle sounds echoing from the bathroom, and the soggy plastic toys dripping from the top of his dresser, that told her the truth.

She glanced up, noticing headlights coming down the driveway.

In the hours Pete and Sam had been gone, she'd related her conversation with Dana—or Miss Simons—to Bob.

"And you let Sam head to town with Pete?" her husband had asked. It was just one sentence, but she knew it held many implications. First, that such behavior shouldn't be rewarded. Second, that Pete, who hadn't finished school himself, wasn't exactly the best influence.

She heard the sounds of Pete's truck parking outside and the voices of Sam and Pete as they unloaded supplies from the back of the truck.

As if also remembering their conversation from earlier that day, Bob's gaze lifted from his Louis L'Amour novel, met Charlotte's gaze, and cocked a bushy gray eyebrow.

"Don't worry." She brushed a hand in the air. "No more outings till the essay is done. I even have plans to stop by the library tomorrow to help Sam find some books on our lovely state . . . after the morning chores, of course."

The rumble of Pete's engine started again. A minute later Sam entered alone, kicking off his tennis shoes by the back door. He had a wrapped foil package in his hands, and a large smile filled his face. "Uncle Pete says he'll be back sometime."

Sam hurried to the fridge and placed what she assumed was leftover pizza on the top shelf, and then he moved to the stairs, most likely heading up to his room.

"Not so fast." Charlotte motioned him to the dining room table. "We need to talk."

He returned, head lowered.

Sam tucked his hands into his baggy jeans pockets and his shoulders slumped. He glanced up, his eyes barely visible under his floppy hair.

He reminded Charlotte of a toddler who had just been

caught with his hand in the cookie jar. She glanced at Bob but he didn't seem quite as amused.

"Sam, aren't you gonna ask what Miss Simons was doing on the farm today?"

Sam lifted his arms, palms up, and shrugged. "Paying a visit to an old friend? Or maybe about Emily?"

She tilted her chin, waiting for a better response.

"Oh, wait. Emily's in the ninth grade and she doesn't have Miss Simons." He lowered his gaze. "So maybe . . . to talk to you about my essay?"

"Yes." She set her needlework on the table. "And just what were you thinking?"

"It's not my fault." His eyes met hers again and his brow furrowed. "She told us to write a nonfiction essay about Nebraska. School only started last week and they already have us writing essays? This place is nuts. Or maybe it's just so boring they think essays are fun. Besides, Miss Simons said to be concise—or whatever that word is. There's nothin' more true or more *concise* than what I wrote."

"And you really thought we'd be okay with this?" Bob put down his book and crossed his arms over his chest. "Do you think disrespect and failure will be allowed? It's not like you're in fourth grade anymore. Being a junior in high school requires responsibility."

Sam's eyes widened as if he realized for the first time that his grandfather was going to back his wife up.

"No, I guess not."

"Good." Charlotte nodded. "Because Miss Simons is giving you a second chance, but this time only."

"You mean I have to write it again?"

"More like *actually write it*. By the end of the month. And it will be longer than the first—four pages. A report on the good things about Nebraska."

Sam's face scrunched in a scowl.

"And it better be the best paper you've ever written," Bob added.

"Yeah, whatever." He retreated, hurrying up the stairs.

Charlotte closed her eyes. Questions and concerns filled her mind. The kids had only been around for a few months. How would she and Bob ever make it until they were grown and gone? Heaviness settled on her, almost pressing her shoulders down. She'd failed the first time. Denise had been a pregnant runaway, and Pete hadn't even graduated. The only one who'd done well was Bill, their oldest son, and he rarely came around. What did that say about her parental achievements? What made her think she'd do a better job this time?

"Maybe you're right. Maybe he doesn't need to hang out with Pete so much . . ." She leaned back on the couch, her interest in needlework diminished.

"Yeah, well, we'll have to keep an eye on that." Bob yawned and rose. "But enough for tonight. I need to hit the hay. Morning comes early, and I need to get the ol' combine fired up. Stupid machine was giving me fits."

Though his words sounded like a complaint, Charlotte knew the truth. The work tired him, but he was happiest when he was in the fields bringing in the harvest. She'd decided long ago that being able to physically reap the rewards for one's hard work was something every man should experience.

"Sure, well, I'm going to get Christopher tucked in and then bid the girls a good-night." Even as she said the words, they still didn't seem part of her reality. It was almost like she was just playing house—even though the kids' presence and their longevity in the household was all too real.

She turned off all the lights, made sure the doors were locked, and headed upstairs. She usually wasn't one to lock the doors, but she had to admit the vegetables missing from the garden bothered her.

Christopher had already dried off, dressed, and climbed into bed when she arrived to say prayers with him and read him a chapter from a book of his choice. Currently, it was *Stuart Little*. Their nightly ritual was a new habit, to be sure, but one they both enjoyed.

"Night." She kissed Christopher's forehead, breathing in his scent that still hinted of "boy," despite the bath. She turned off the light and closed the door so that it was open just a crack.

Charlotte turned to Emily's room. The door was ajar, and she paused in the doorway. Instead of the loud laughter from a minute before, the girls were lying on their backs on the carpet. Their faces, with blue eye shadow and pink lipstick, gave evidence of makeovers. Each girl's leg was propped in the air as she painted her toes. Charlotte had never seen anyone paint her toenails like that, but she was even more intrigued by their conversation.

"I just don't get it." Emily blew as if her breath could reach the wet paint on her toes. "I don't get it why you call Pepsi and stuff 'pop.' Rice Krispies pop, soda doesn't."

"Yeah, well, when you say *soda*, I think of baking soda— you know the kind you use when you're baking a cake."

"No. I've never used that stuff."

Ashley lifted her head slightly. "You're kiddin'! You've never baked a cake?"

"Of course I've baked a cake. The mixes I've used never called for anything called *soda*."

"You make *boxed* cake?" Ashley's voice was no more than a loud whisper. Her face appeared horrified, as if Emily had just announced she'd robbed a bank.

"Yeah, well, maybe we didn't have time in California to make stuff from scratch because we had too much fun stuff —like the beach and mall and arcades. There were even mountains to hike, and my mom used to take us there."

With the mention of Denise, both girls quieted. Charlotte took a step back, realizing they still hadn't seen her.

Emily cleared her throat. "Yeah, well, like I was saying, I don't know why anyone would want to stay in Nebraska forever. There is no ocean, no mountains, not to mention all the potholes and no place to shop."

"I don't know. I kind of like it. I like raising lambs. I like 4-H. I like being able to hang out at Heather Creek all day without having to worry about car-jackings and stuff."

"Let's just agree to disagree." Emily's voice was firm. "As soon as I'm old enough, I'm out of here, just like Sam. Nothing here worth keeping me around."

The words jabbed Charlotte's heart like a butcher's knife.

Just like your mom.

"I'll be sad if you do . . . but at least it will give me someplace to visit. I've never been to San Diego."

She'd heard enough. Charlotte cleared her throat and entered. "Okay, girls, time for bed."

She hugged her waist, pretending she hadn't heard, and offered her best smile. "After your polish is dry, of course."

Emily sat up, startled. She looked at Charlotte, her gaze filled with questions. Charlotte glanced away.

"Christopher has gone to bed and I suggest you do the same. Morning will come soon." She turned and exited, realizing that she hadn't prayed with Emily, as she had just started doing. But for the life of her she couldn't make herself return to that room. Instead Emily's words replayed in her mind.

Nothing here worth keeping me around.

Chapter
Eight

Charlotte woke up to the sound of the combine sputtering in the barn. She rose and padded to the window, gazing out into the predawn darkness. The window was slightly ajar, and the cool wind brushed against her bare arms, causing goose bumps to rise on her skin. She rubbed her arms, sending up a silent prayer that the old combine would start. Bob didn't need the stress and struggle. With each false start she could imagine his blood pressure rising.

Tilting her head to look to the front, she noticed Pete's truck wasn't out there.

"Now where is that boy?"

There were times he went out and played pool at a friend's house or stayed up watching those guy movies that were high in action and minimal in story line. He never got into big trouble, but he didn't always make the wisest choices either.

She hadn't seen Pete after he'd dropped off Sam, and she had a feeling he was up to something. Charlotte dressed quickly. The clock read 6:45 AM, and the first rays of pink sunlight peeked over the tree break east of the house. The house was quiet, and she decided to let the kids sleep a little longer.

She wished at times like this Pete had a cell phone. Not that it would do any good if he was anywhere on the farm. But if he was in town perhaps she could reach him.

She was thinking about calling Pete's friend from the feed store when she noticed headlights coming down the road. She crossed her arms over her chest and walked out to the front porch. Toby wasn't there to greet her, and Charlotte assumed she was in the barn with Bob.

She imagined Bob was venting steam as he worked on the combine. Most likely mad at the old machine for not starting, and even madder at Pete for not being around to help. Still, what could she say to her son? Pete was too old to be scolded. He worked the farm from sunup to sundown with very little pay. Sometimes it was hard for both her and Bob to remember Pete had his own life beyond the farm. In fact, maybe it was the farm that hindered him from having his own family too.

Charlotte turned to go back into the white, clapboard house when she noticed more vehicles following Pete's truck.

Her hand moved to her throat as she saw Pete wasn't returning alone. From the looks of it, he wouldn't be working alone either. Two large combines, two work trucks, and a grain truck followed Pete's truck as he turned onto their long gravel driveway.

A knot tightened in her stomach. She stepped back into the house and hurried to the dining room, where she sank into one of the high-backed wooden chairs. Her hands folded and unfolded on her lap as she realized the truth of what her son was up to.

Pete, you wouldn't...Don't tell me you did. Don't tell me you went off and hired a crew.

From her seat, she watched through the window as the vehicles approached. The engine sounds combined and grew, roaring like angry thunder that sometimes filled the Nebraska sky. She reached for her embroidery basket, which she'd left on the table.

Footsteps sounded behind her. Heavy footsteps jogging down the stairs. She didn't need to turn to see who it was.

The footsteps reached the bottom.

"Sam."

"Yeah, Grandma?"

"You know anything about this? About what's happening outside the window?"

She picked a piece of embroidery thread the same color of green as the combines pulling into her driveway, and twisted it around her finger. She listened as Sam walked to the door and slid his feet into the work boots handed down from Pete.

"You mean the combine crew?"

"That's exactly what I mean."

"Uncle Pete saw them yesterday. They were in town and the neighbor—I can't remember the name—wasn't ready for them. They gave Uncle Pete a good deal 'cause they didn't want to waste the trip to Bedford."

"Is that the true story? Or is it just the one you've been told to tell?"

Sam frowned but didn't respond, and Charlotte rose and

turned. Pain shot through her temples, and she attempted to rub away the tightness of her forehead with her fingertips.

The tall boy pulled his jacket off the hook by the back door, and shrugged it on. "Uncle Pete's just worried about Grandpa, that's all. With his health, you know."

"Yes, I know." She patted Sam's shoulder. "You go ahead. I'll be right out." She heard shouts from outside. Bob's shouts. "On second thought, why don't you wait here a minute? Give me a chance to talk to Grandpa first."

Charlotte put on her own work boots and quickly tied them. She tugged on a sweater and hurried outside. Pete's truck was parked in its usual spot, and she guessed from the shouting that he'd already found his way into the barn. The combines and trucks had stopped farther down the driveway. She offered a quick wave to the men now gathering outside their rigs and then hurried to the barn.

Bob and Pete stood just inside the door. They'd lowered their voices, but their words still rumbled with emotion.

"And where did you get the money for this?" Bob paced back and forth in front of Pete. "That work account is for things we need around the farm. Things we can't live without. I don't even want to think of what you've paid for something we could've done ourselves. Something I've been taking care of just fine for the past forty years!"

Pete stood with his hands in jeans pockets, unmoving. Charlotte's heart filled with empathy at the sight of his slumped shoulders and lowered head. It was the same stance he'd had since he was four and got caught sneaking vegetables from the garden, taking them to feed the ponies at a neighboring farm. He'd grown up, and still was rough around the edges, but deep down she knew he was just a kid wanting to help his dad.

"I talked to Bill. He agreed—"

"So you're *both* in on this?" Bob interrupted.

"Well, I just wanted to talk to someone and make sure I was doing the right thing. I knew—"

"You didn't think you could talk to me?" Bob's hand slammed against the metal door of the combine. "Thought your brother, who hardly sets foot on this place, would know what to do better than your old man?"

"Bob..." Charlotte approached and placed a hand on his shoulder.

He stopped pacing, but the words continued. "I don't need their help. I've been harvesting by myself all my life. And now some know-it-all kid..."

"Bob." Charlotte's voice rose.

"Dad, listen, I knew you wouldn't be happy, but I also knew that if you tried to do it all yourself, it would kill you. I'm only one person. I can't drive the combine and the grain truck too." He turned to Charlotte. "Tell him, Mom. Tell him that he needs to take it easy."

Pete turned back to Bob, his shoulders squaring with determination. "Sure, the profit won't be as big, but who's gonna take care of Mom and the kids if you keel over dead?"

Bob turned to Charlotte, his eyes intent on hers. He pushed his hands deep into the front pockets of his overalls. "So you were in on this too?"

"No, but if Pete talked to Bill...and well, he's right about all the work. And the old combine isn't what it used to be. If Pete got a good deal . . ." She bit her lip, refusing to bring up the subject of Bob's health. He hadn't wanted to hear it before, and he surely didn't now.

"Listen, Dad." Pete pointed a thumb outside. "Those new machines, they work twice as fast as our old one. And the crew, they're a good bunch of guys. They take care of everything. It's a good deal."

"Good deal?" Bob removed his hand from his pocket and hit it against his thigh. "Why, it's plumb foolishness paying someone to do the work when there's a perfectly fine machine in this barn."

"A fine machine that doesn't run?" It was Sam's voice, and Charlotte glanced up, for the first time noticing he'd followed her out.

Bob pointed his chin in Sam's direction. "Oh, and so now *everyone* else knows more about this than me? Everyone has a better idea how to run a farm?" Bob readjusted his cap on his head. "Well, good, then they can just have at it. If everyone else thinks they know best, then they don't need my help." With long steps he strode off, exiting the barn, walking angrily around the corner in the direction of Heather Creek.

Charlotte glanced from Pete to Sam, and then back to Pete again. She let out a helpless sigh. "You know how your father gets. He doesn't mean those things—he just gets angry. Not just at you, but angry at what he can't do anymore."

"Nothing I didn't expect. He still sees me as a snotty-nosed kid. Doesn't understand that it's for his own good."

"I know." She buttoned her sweater buttons, slowly, deliberately, trying to find the right words. "But I see his point too. I mean, I'm sure it's going to be a lot of money. Those men out there have mouths to feed back home. They have to pay for those machines. It's not like we have all that much saved up. We're going to need every penny. With the kids here—" She touched Pete's arm.

Pete jerked his arm away. "Yeah, like I said, nothing I didn't expect. First the rant, then the lecture."

Pete lowered his head and hurried out of the barn.

Charlotte opened her mouth to call him back, but realized he was right. Sam stood there, not saying a word. He turned and watched as Pete approached the crew, smiling and shaking each man's hand as if the last ten minutes hadn't just happened.

"Can I . . ." Sam stopped short. "I told Uncle Pete I'd help . . ." He looked at her as if uncertain if he should even ask.

"Go ahead, get. Pete's gonna need you. Don't worry about Grandpa. I'll take care of him."

Sam nodded and then jogged toward Pete. It was only after he'd reached the others—looking more like a man by just being with them—that she remembered about the library and the report. She'd planned on helping him pick out books, but now Sam would most likely be in the fields all day. No doubt Bob would again make his point about Pete's influence.

"Dear Lord, we need your help most desperately today." She folded her arms across her chest and hugged them close, feeling a mix of thankfulness and angst over the big machines outside. One of the barn cats meowed and approached, weaving in and out of her legs, and in a strange way reminding her that they would get past this day like they had all the rest. If God cared for scraggly little barn cats, didn't God care for them too?

"Please help Bob to understand. Help Pete to be patient and kind, not trying to do too much too fast. They're so busy making their own case, they refuse to listen. They . . ." She paused. "And not just them, Lord, me too. It seems we're all set in our old patterns and habits around here. I think these kids are here for a reason—" She watched as Sam and Pete eyed one of the large combines, talking with the driver. "To mix things up. To make us rethink our old ways." Charlotte sighed. "And to keep us coming to You."

CHARLOTTE FOUND HERSELF down on her knees in the kitchen, this time wiping up a spot of something that had dribbled down the cabinet, pooled on the floor, and hardened. *Where is that cat when I really need him?*

From the large, empty yogurt container in the trash and the pink goop she was scrubbing, she imagined what the pink stuff was—a midnight snack. Someone had gotten up and made something to eat during the night. Strawberry yogurt . . . and the half-dozen oatmeal cookies she was sure had been in the bottom of the cookie jar when she went to bed last night.

Girls' voices carried down the stairs and "the Lees"—as Bob had started calling Ashley and Emily—entered the kitchen.

"Grandma, we're heading out to feed the horses and gather the eggs. Then we're going to town, right?" Emily twisted her light hair up on her head and worked a rubber band around it, making a ponytail. She pulled the ponytail tight, adjusted a ball cap on her head, and pulled the tail through the opening in the back.

Charlotte forced herself not to smirk at the skintight jeans the girl wore. But at least the large T-shirt and sweatshirt over that made Emily look like a typical Nebraska teen.

"Yeah, that's right." With a grunt and a groan, Charlotte picked herself up off the floor. "And while you're at it, can you walk down the road and check the fence near the far pasture? Hannah called last night and said one of the posts was leaning—needs to be fixed—and I just want to make sure the cows won't get out." Hannah Carter was Charlotte's neighbor and good friend. "I can't imagine anything worse than those combines losing a good day's work because the cows got in the soybeans."

"Sure, and then are we going to town?"

"That's the plan."

The girls clapped as if she'd just announced they were heading to the county fair. Charlotte watched as Ashley threaded her arm into Emily's cocked elbow, and they headed out. Her heart warmed at the sight. Because the truth was, even if she and Bob lost most of the money in the bank, even if the men on the farm were having their own private war, Emily had found a friend—a good friend and a good influence—and that was one bright spot in the otherwise challenging day.

That and the fact it *was* harvest. No matter who brought in the soybeans, and no matter who would follow up with the corn next month, the Lord had provided greatly. The weather had been all they could have asked for. And they'd faced the months since Denise's death with God's help. More than that, the kids seemed to be adjusting, and that was a harvest blessing all its own.

She opened the butter-yellow cupboard and scanned the contents inside, knowing that what the men did outside was the very thing that kept these cupboards full.

From the mail pile on the counter, she grabbed a now-empty envelope from the electric bill and scribbled down the items she needed to pick up at the store.

Protein powder for smoothies, bread, peanut butter, macaroni. She thought about adding flour and cocoa powder to the list, for a cake, but realized she had no time to make one.

She scribbled on her envelope and tried to keep her mind focused on her trip to town instead of the drama of this morning. But no matter how hard she tried to focus, her stomach churned as she wondered what Bob was doing. *How he was doing.* She glanced out the window, wondering where he had gone. Wondering if it would be better if she just kept up with the normal plans for her day or if she should head out and look for him.

If it were her, she'd want someone to come and find her. She'd want someone to talk it over with. Yet Bob was different. He processed all his thoughts, feelings, and emotions inside his head and rarely wanted to "talk things out." Perhaps it was due to the fact that most of the time farming was a solitary occupation. He spent hours alone planting, harvesting, feeding. Maybe he'd just gotten used to letting his mind work out the problems as his body worked at its assigned task.

Charlotte had just finished adding cleaning supplies and dog food to the list when Emily and Ashley rushed in. Ashley carried Emily's egg bucket and held it out in front for Charlotte to peer into.

"Mrs. Stevenson, guess what! The chicks you bought a few months ago have laid their first eggs. Look!"

Charlotte smiled at the girl's dancing eyes and her flushed and freckled cheeks. She only wished Emily would be as excited about the chore. Even after all these months, Emily hated the chickens—or rather hated the smell of the chickens.

"Why, you're right, Ashley." Charlotte pulled a brown egg off the top of the pile. "It's a pullet egg."

"A what?" Emily wrinkled her nose.

Ashley held out her hand, and Charlotte placed the brown egg in her palm—the only place on Ashley's body without freckles. "*Pullet* is another name for a young hen. And because they're still little, the eggs are too."

"See?" Ashley moved over to the kitchen window and held the egg up to the sunlight so Emily could get a better look. "They're smaller, a nice brown, and smoother than regular eggs."

Emily took it from her and turned the egg in her hand, inspecting it in the light, like a jeweler examining a diamond. "It almost looks shiny."

Charlotte marveled that Emily seemed almost interested in the egg.

Almost.

With a shrug, Emily placed the egg in the bucket and then moved to the fridge, rearranging the eggs in the cardboard carrier so that the newer, fresher ones were in the back. Not that Charlotte had to worry much anymore about food going bad. There were enough hungry stomachs around to make sure that didn't happen.

Emily finished adjusting all the eggs and then picked the small brown one up to look at it again. "How long will they stay like this?"

"Oh, a month or so, give or take."

"Do they taste the same?" Emily asked.

"Just like any other egg. Want me to whip a few up in an omelet?"

Emily shrugged, and Charlotte took that as a yes. It wasn't a steak dinner, but it was a start.

"It's a good thing these youngsters have begun laying," she commented nonchalantly as she cracked the eggs, whipped them, and added a little fresh milk for fluffiness. "The eggs from the old hens are getting fewer and far between, and sometimes it seems like Sam goes through a dozen eggs by himself."

"He likes them fried at breakfast," Emily informed Ashley. "And Christopher likes scrambled."

As if responding to his name, the boy's voice carried down the stairs. "Grandma, look! Did you see outside?" His blue pajamas were decorated with a large Spider-Man face, and Christopher's wide-eyed look was fixed on the machines outside.

"Where did they come from? What are they doing? Are they going to be here all day? Can I ride one?" The questions came so fast Charlotte waved her hand in front of her mouth, motioning for Christopher to breathe.

Christopher sucked in a deep breath. He blew it out slowly, and then smiled. "Can I?"

"Tell you what. Let me finish with my list and then I'll take you out and show you around. That should give you time to get dressed and cleaned up."

Christopher didn't respond. Instead he turned and hurried back up the stairs, his footsteps pounding on each step.

Chapter Nine

His grandma wasn't in the kitchen when he finished dressing, so Christopher headed outside to wait. In the field across the gravel driveway, two large machines moved in straight lines, driving over the soybean plants and gobbling them up like big, hungry, green beetles.

Christopher watched the machines and something inside his stomach jumped and danced. It was the coolest thing he'd ever seen.

Large black-and-yellow tires rolled around and around, and though they were far away in the field, he was sure the tires stood taller than him. On the side of the machine was a ladder with big steps leading up to a window box that reminded him of the glass elevator at that fancy mall his mom used to like to go to. One man sat in the high seat, with glass all around him, steering the big machine.

"I wanna do that some day," Christopher muttered. Though no one was in hearing distance, he repeated himself. "I wanna drive that big combine thing when I get older."

The black cutter on the front of the machine was wide enough to sweep over lots of those little soybean rows at one time. The cutter looked like a cake beater on its side, spinning and spinning. The cutter was held by two large arms. In the field, the combine finished one row and did a U-turn to the next.

When the combine turned, the cutter arms lifted like the arms of a robot. The rumble of the combine even sounded like a spaceship lifting up. No wonder the aliens liked this place. If he were an alien, he would have picked Nebraska too.

Most of the cut-grass stuff fell flat, tumbling under the blade and getting run over by the machine. But from his view, Christopher saw that some of the stalks refused to fall and instead jumped and danced over the blade, hitting the glass window and falling down again into the cutter.

Christopher glanced at the white house behind him and decided it would be okay to venture across the driveway to get a closer look. He would still be in yelling distance, and just as long as he didn't go into the field, he would be fine.

A cloud of fine dust poured out from behind the machine, a light brown cloud. A long arm stuck out on the side of the green machine as if to signal that it was making a left-hand turn, just like his mom taught him to do when he was riding his bicycle on the street.

He could hear footsteps crunching on the gravel behind him. He glanced back and saw his grandpa standing there, watching the large machine. His grandpa's eyes looked sad, and Christopher wondered if Grandpa wished he was out there driving one of them.

"Grandpa, what's that arm thing? Is it like a vacuum that will bend down and suck up the soybeans?"

"Actually, the soybeans get sucked inside, underneath."

"After they're cut off?" Christopher watched the machine, eyeing the blades.

"Yup, the blade cuts off the grain and part of the plant. Then those pieces enter the combine. Inside they rub between two pieces of metal called the separator."

"Do they separate the bad stuff from the good stuff?"

His grandpa chuckled. He rubbed his chin and nodded. "Do you mean separate the grain from the plant material? Why, yes, they do."

"Then the grain goes into the bin in the back?"

"Not quite. Inside there are also two screens and a big fan underneath. The fan lifts most of the plant parts off the grain and blows them out the back of the combine. That's the chaffer. Then the grain runs over a second screen, called a sieve, and all the grain falls through the holes and then—"

"It's dumped into the back?" Christopher squinted as he looked at the machine and tried to picture all the pieces in his mind.

"Actually, it's not dumped. After the other stuff is taken away, the grain is augered into that big bin right behind the cab where the driver sits."

"Aug, aug . . . huh?" Christopher scratched his head.

"Augered. It's like—" His grandpa glanced behind him, past the house, and then toward the tractor shed. "I know, come with me." His grandpa led the way to the tractor shed and made his way to his workbench.

Inside the house Grandma had lots of stuff everywhere

that was pretty to look at. Grandpa's space had a lot of stuff, but everything was lined up and labeled, and he guessed that if anyone took anything Grandpa would know exactly what was missing and where it was missing from.

On the worktable were old coffee cans, each one with a white sticker labeled for screws, bolts, hinges . . . Suddenly, Christopher wondered if Grandpa knew about *everything* that was in the tractor shed. He worried that Grandpa had found the old metal part that he'd hidden behind the bucket. Christopher decided to come out later and check. One thing was for sure: He didn't want to lose his treasure.

Grandpa picked up the coffee can labeled *Screws* and took one out, holding it up for Christopher.

"See the way this little lip wraps around the screw from the bottom to the top?"

He eyed it and nodded.

"Well, imagine the screw top wasn't there and the rest of this screw was positioned inside a tube." He turned the screw in his fingers, around and around. "The auger is like that, and when it turns, it carries the grain from the bottom to the top on this lip."

"Sort of like a dizzy elevator."

"Exactly like a dizzy elevator."

His grandpa placed the screw in his hand. Christopher moved his finger from the bottom to the top of the screw, winding it. "Around, around, around, and up to the top."

"Yeah, so once all the grain has been separated from the plant parts, it moves up the auger into a big bin that sits behind the cab of the combine. When the bin gets full it gets dumped into the grain truck, and the truck dumps it into grain bins to dry or into the grain elevator to be stored."

"Cool. I never knew about combines before." Christopher tossed the screw back into the can and his grandpa put the lid back on it and placed it back on the workbench.

"For many years I drove one, but my old combine isn't what it used to be."

"Do you think I can drive one of those when I get older?"

"I'm sure you can," his grandpa answered.

"And two combines will make the harvest go faster?"

"Two . . . and the fact that they are newer machines."

"Well, when I get older, we can get two new combines. I'll drive one and you can drive one."

Grandpa's eyes got that sad look again.

"Okay, sport, we'll do that. Now it's time for you to get inside and get some breakfast. But feed the cats first."

"Okay, Grandpa."

He moved to the door, imagining the furry cats all running toward him when they heard him pour the cat food into their big dish. Except for Lightning. Lightning had his own dish in the house. Christopher put his hand on the doorknob to open the door.

"Christopher, wait."

He turned and saw his grandpa holding a toy tractor in his hand.

"I remembered I had this in here. It used to be Pete's when he was about your age."

"Really?" Christopher's eyes were wide. "Can I play with it?"

"Sure, I don't see why not."

"Cool. It looks just about the right size to give the cats a ride."

And with that he took it from his grandpa's hands and rushed to the barn, deciding that he could wait until later to check on his treasure, 'cause he was sure the cats never rode a tractor before.

Chapter Ten

"C hristopher?" Charlotte called up the stairs, wiping her hands on her apron. Partly for therapy and partly out of necessity, she was in the middle of peeling apples for applesauce. She *did* have a lot of apples in the cellar that she needed to do something with, and she didn't want to head into town until she had talked with Bob. Surely he would come back to the house. He couldn't spend the whole day wandering the farm deep in thought.

"Christopher," she called louder. "Are you up there?"

There was no answer.

"Emily?" Charlotte turned to the two girls making ham and cheese sandwiches for the workers. Emily had come up with the idea of an assembly line with pieces of bread lined up from one end of the long table to the other.

Emily paused from spreading mustard on the pieces. "Yeah, Grandma?"

"Have you seen Christopher? I thought he was upstairs getting dressed, but he's not answering me."

"He ran outside when you were down in the cellar."

"And you didn't tell me?"

Emily shrugged. "I didn't know you wanted to know."

A cold fear gripped Charlotte's heart. She pushed the screen door open and ran toward the grain bin.

"Christopher!" Her voice split the air. Charlotte felt a sharp pain in her chest and her knees trembled as she hurried toward the gravity wagon. "Christopher." *Please, Lord, please, Lord, please keep him safe.*

Charlotte had told herself last night to make sure in the morning to give Christopher, Emily, and even Sam the safety talk. She didn't know why she hadn't thought about it sooner. From the time Bill, Denise, and Pete were toddlers, she had reminded them over and over what *not* to touch, or climb on, or hide under. By the time they were Christopher's age, they'd known the rules by heart. A farm was a wonderful place to live, work, and grow up, but it wasn't without its dangers. Every year many kids were killed in farm accidents. She'd read all about the accidents in the newspaper. In the night she'd reminded herself to talk to them, but her good intentions quickly got pushed out by the conflict between Pete and Bob. *Why didn't I make sure to give him the talk? To tell him about all the dangers?*

"Christopher!"

She reached the red gravity wagon that looked similar to a grain car on a train. It was tall with large wheels and a door on the side. It was through that door that the grain emptied into the bins. A ladder led to the open top. It was the ladder that troubled Charlotte. More than one neighbor child had drowned in the grain after falling in. She moved to the ladder, gripping the middle rung.

"Grandma?"

"Christopher!" Charlotte turned and saw Christopher. Lightning wiggled in his hands.

"You weren't going to climb up there, were you, Grandma? 'Cause Uncle Pete says it's not safe."

She noticed a toy tractor on the ground. He dropped to his knees and held the cat on top. "See, he likes to drive."

Christopher moved the tractor a foot forward, just enough out of reach for the cat to escape. Laughter burst from Charlotte, both from relief and humor at Christopher's wide-eyed gaze at his disappearing playmate.

"So Uncle Pete gave you the talk, huh?"

"Yup. A few days ago. He said things can be dangerous around harvest. No climbing on machines. No climbing under 'em. No climbing in them. He said to always listen to that little voice."

"Little voice?" Charlotte squatted down before him.

"The one that says, 'I wonder if this is a good idea.' Uncle Pete says if you have to ask, then it's *not* a good idea."

"That is very good advice."

Christopher rose and asked his grandma, "Were you lookin' for me?"

Charlotte felt better knowing that Christopher was safe, but she still had an unsettled feeling, wondering what had happened to Bob. She saw Christopher studying her face and she forced a smile.

"Well, I'm taking Emily and Ashley to town. Do you wanna come?"

"Can we get a treat?"

"I'm sure we can."

"And are we going to the library?"

"How did you know about that?"

"I heard you telling Sam, and I want to get some books on machines and stuff."

Charlotte looked at the toy. "Like tractors?"

Christopher nodded enthusiastically. "Yeah, like that . . . and other machines."

"Sure, but I need to find Grandpa first. Then we'll go." Charlotte scanned the farm, letting her gaze sweep across the fields where the combines worked, across the pasture with the cows, but she didn't spot Bob anywhere.

She glanced to the barn, wondering if he'd made his way back in there to tinker with the old combine again.

"You need to find him? Do you think Grandpa wants to go too?"

"Do you know where he is?"

"He's in the tractor shed. Before that he was watching the combines in the field. He told me how they work. He said I might be able to drive one when I get older. He looked kind of sad, though. So maybe he wants a treat too."

"Your grandpa has been farming for many years. I'm sure he doesn't quite know what to do with himself now that . . ." Charlotte let her words fade. Christopher didn't need to know the details. *Let him think about toy tractors and cats and treats while he can. He'll be forced to grow up all too soon.*

"Hey." She slapped her leg. "I think you had a good idea. Can you ask Grandpa if he wants to come? Tell him that I need help loading the groceries."

"Sure!" Christopher raced to the tractor shed.

"Meet you in the house," Charlotte called after him. She whispered a silent prayer that Bob would cooperate.

Then she hurried back to the house. The girls had finished making the sandwiches and were wrapping them to be taken to the crew.

Charlotte placed her apples in the refrigerator to finish later and watched out the window for Bob. With Christopher chatting away by his side, he strolled toward the house, as he did every day. From his expression, it was hard to tell what he was thinking. Was he still angry?

Bob wiped off his boots and entered the house. Charlotte turned with a smile.

"We're going to town?" Bob changed from his work jacket to his town jacket.

"I thought you could help me with the groceries. Unless you were going to help unload the beans?"

"Nah, Pete's gonna teach Sam to empty the grain wagon."

"They're not taking it to the elevator?"

"Guess not. Pete thinks the beans are still too moist. He's going to let them dry in the bin before he takes them in. Thinks they'll get a better price."

"Sounds like you taught him well."

"Everyone ready?" Bob said, ignoring her comment.

"Yeah, the sandwiches and snacks are ready. We can take them out to the field on our way out."

"Girls, let's go." Bob took his keys from the hook by the door. "Christopher is already waiting in the car."

"Do you want us to take the sandwiches?" Emily slipped on her shoes. Ashley did the same.

"No, I'll take care of it." Bob's voice was gruff.

Without a word, the girls hurried outside. Bob grabbed up the plastic bags with the food.

Charlotte touched his arm.

He paused and turned to her.

"You okay?"

"Why wouldn't I be okay?"

"Oh, maybe because this is the first time in forty years you haven't been out there with the soybeans?"

Bob grunted, then he strode out the door and walked outside. He didn't need words to show his displeasure.

Charlotte looked around the kitchen at the mess of crumbs and wrappers the girls had left everywhere. Normally she would clean it up before she left, but she knew that when Bob was ready to go somewhere, he was ready to go.

She slipped on her jacket, grabbed her purse, and then waited outside. Bob was leaving the food on the hood of Pete's truck.

She placed her hands on her hips and shook her head. But at least he wasn't yelling. At least he wasn't moping. She just hoped that when they got home things wouldn't blow up again.

Just a little peace, dear Lord. Can we have a little peace, a little acceptance, please?

Chapter
Eleven

The scent of Edna's talcum, mixed with musty books, greeted Charlotte's nose as they entered the library. Since the kids had first come to live at the farm, Edna had bugged Charlotte about getting them into town and getting them library cards. At the grocery store, at church, anyplace they happened to meet, Edna would urge Charlotte to get them to the library, as if signing their name on the small piece of plastic would transform everything and be the one thing to make them feel like a part of the small community.

"Welcome!" Edna puckered her lips with approval. Her face was round and her dyed black hair was short. It framed her face as if she'd brushed it forward and then sprayed it so that it stuck to her cheeks.

Edna smiled wide. "I had a feeling that today would be the day, with the guys busy with the harvest and . . ." Edna's words stopped short when she saw Bob enter after Charlotte. "Like I was saying," she continued hurriedly, "come here, young man, and you show me just what types of books you're interested in."

"Books with machines. *All* types of machines—driving machines, *flying* machines."

"Sure thing, young man."

Edna turned to Emily and Ashley. "And when I'm done with this young man, I'll help you two."

The girls' eyes widened, and they looked at each other. "Thanks, but I think we'll just check out the magazines today," Ashley said, tugging on Emily's arm and leading her to the large bin where used magazines were brought in for others to enjoy.

Edna's face fell, and she was obviously disappointed she couldn't put her book knowledge to work helping them too. Still, Edna squared her shoulders and nodded, leading Christopher to the nonfiction section with great strides of importance.

Charlotte noticed the first magazines Emily picked up were the teen ones with photos of the most current movie stars plastered on the glossy cover. *Of course.*

Ashley was no better, flipping through a fashion magazine where the models wore clothes that cost more than Charlotte's car.

Bob glanced around, studying the place. "So what did you need in here? More of those cookbooks you like so well? Maybe a new cookie recipe?" Bob rubbed his stomach.

"Actually, I was thinking of picking up some books for Sam's report. I think there's a whole Nebraska shelf around here—"

"I don't think so."

"What do you mean?"

"It's Sam's report. Sam can get his own books."

"But he's helping Pete."

"That's his choice."

"And if I don't get them now it will mean another trip into town—for me."

Bob opened his mouth again, then closed it. He glanced toward Emily and Ashley, whose gazes were intent on them.

"Fine, just hurry. I'm getting a little hungry—I think these girls are too. Girls, why don't you wait outside on the bench while I help with these books?" Bob pointed to the park bench positioned in front of the library.

They nodded and tossed their magazines back into the bin, then hurried outside.

He turned back to Charlotte. "Go get what you need for Sam. *If* you think it's best . . ."

Charlotte nodded, then moved among the rows of books. The knot in her stomach from this morning's events cinched tighter and tighter with each step. Maybe Bob was right. Maybe she was making things too easy for Sam. Someday soon he'd have to figure out this stuff on his own. After all, it wouldn't be long before he was old enough to move out and make his own decisions. Then what?

Charlotte scanned the aisles and soon found the shelf with books on Nebraska. Her hand trembled as she reached for one and paused. *Sam needs help*, she told herself. *He's been through a lot. Besides, I really don't have time to make another trip into town this week . . .*

Pinching her lower lip between her teeth, she picked out a half dozen that she thought would interest Sam. She carried them to the front and noticed Christopher already waiting with a large stack in his arms.

"Wow, it looks like you found a little reading material," Bob commented.

"Not to mention these." Edna patted a second pile on the counter.

Charlotte's jaw drop. "Are you serious?"

"Dead serious." Edna pulled out a new library card from the drawer and scanned it. Then she opened the book at the top and slid its barcode under the scanner. The machine beeped, telling them the book had been checked out. Then she moved to the next. Her smile seemed to widen with each book that passed from one pile to the next. "Looks like you have a reader here. Good thing you came in for that card."

Charlotte walked to the counter and placed the Nebraska books next to Christopher's stack. "Are you sure he can check out this many? There must be thirty books here."

"Of course. There's no checkout limit. We don't want to do anything to hinder reading."

Charlotte glanced at the titles.

Bob nodded with a smile. "Trains, planes, and automobiles. Okeydokey."

Edna finished scanning the pile and then loaded the books into plastic bags.

"Do you need me to fill out an application or something for Christopher's card?"

"Nope. I'll just add him to the Stevenson family account." She typed on the computer keyboard. "Yes, here it is. Opened in 1975, the same year the new library opened. Charlotte, Billy, Den—" Edna paused as if realizing what she was about to say. Her eyes widened, and she turned toward

Christopher. "Your mother. I remember her coming in. When she was young she loved to read."

"She did?"

Edna nodded, brushing her hair forward as if trying to distract herself from the trembling of her lower lip.

"I like to read, just like my mom," Christopher proclaimed.

The door opened and Allison Cunningham entered. Charlotte felt her jaw tighten, and she could feel Bob bristle up beside her. More than once that woman's mouth—and her joy in spreading the latest nugget of gossip—had caused Charlotte's family pain. Still, Charlotte offered a quick wave. Edna did too.

"Oh, and I bet Mrs. Cunningham remembers your mother too," Edna told Christopher. "She is so good about updating me on the local kids who have graduated and moved on —those out there seeing the world. That woman's mind is like a steel trap."

Bob leaned his mouth close to Charlotte's ear. "Yeah, just like a steel trap, rusty and dangerous."

Laughter burst from Charlotte's lips and she elbowed Bob.

Edna looked at Bob and Charlotte, her look telling them she wanted in on the private joke. But when they didn't 'fess up, Edna turned her attention back to Christopher. "Oh, one more thing. I need you to sign your card."

Christopher signed the library card and then slipped it into his pocket with a grin.

Charlotte squeezed Christopher's shoulder, and she finally felt she'd done something right by bringing him in here. Even though her intentions had been to help Sam, she was pleased to see Christopher so excited about books and reading. "You just made my day. I never thought a pile of books could make me so happy."

"They're just books, Grandma."

"You may think that now, but to me they're a whole world of opportunities . . ."

"Or maybe out-of-this-world opportunities," Christopher said, grabbing one of the plastic bags and hurrying outside to where the girls waited. Bob grabbed two more bags.

"Let me guess," Charlotte picked the fourth and fifth plastic bags full of books. "Are some of these books on spacecraft and UFOs too?"

"Just a few." Edna walked around the checkout counter and opened the front door.

"Just . . . my whole shelf," Edna added with a wink.

Charlotte laughed as she exited. The two plastic bags tugged on her arms, but her heart felt amazingly light.

CHARLOTTE LET BOB LOAD THE BOOKS into the truck while she convinced the others to make a quick trip to the grocery store before stopping at Mel's Place for a treat.

Now with the grocery bags lined up in the back of the truck, and the week's receipt totaling nearly as much as they used to spend in a month, they headed over to Mel's Place.

Bob walked with short, quick steps like he always did when he was deep in thought, and she was sure he was. The combine crew. The trip to town. Getting books for Sam. Who knew what churned through his mind? She quickened her pace to keep up with his.

She slid her hand into his and squeezed. His hand hung

in hers like a dead fish, and she hoped they could make it through the rest of the day with no more incidents. The sooner this day was over the better.

"You wanna get a cinnamon roll?" She glanced up at him and spoke with a light, cheerful tone.

"My mom makes a fresh batch on Saturday," Ashley said. "They're my favorite. Emily, do you want to share one?"

"And I'll share one with Grandpa," Charlotte said.

Charlotte noticed a slight smile curl Bob's lips, and she knew it brightened his day to get her permission. But she also made a mental note to remind him to check his blood sugar when they got back to the farm.

They entered the restaurant and the cheery atmosphere was like a breath of fresh air. The walls were painted a pale yellow and healthy plants hung from hooks on the wall. Charlotte glanced around, noticing Melody had added some new antiques. All the things that woman accomplished— running a business, taking care of a family, having time for her friends, *and* taking time to go above and beyond to make her place look nice—amazed Charlotte.

Familiar faces sat around the wooden tables, and on the tables, straw-scarecrow centerpieces smiled at the diners.

Local art hung on the walls, and Charlotte recognized landscape scenes painted by an older lady who attended their church, but the art wasn't what caught her attention. She breathed in the scent of fresh baked goods and coffee, and turned her attention to the glass case that displayed muffins and pies and other desserts.

The door had hardly shut behind them when Charlotte saw Melody rise from one of the booths just inside the door. She wore a bright orange shirt covered with even brighter spring flowers. On anyone else such a shirt would look like a walking flower stand, but on Melody it simply accentuated her bright smile.

"Well, look here. Just the family I was hoping to see today." Melody's arms circled Charlotte and pulled her into a warm hug.

Charlotte patted Melody's back and smiled. "Yes, well, we can't make a trip to town without stopping for a special treat."

Melody stepped back, patted Bob's arm and offered him a smile and then turned to the kids. "And how are the youngins? Not causing too much trouble, I hope. Ashley, did you mind your manners?"

Ashley nodded.

"Of course she did," Charlotte said. "Ashley's a joy to have around."

"Good, then I suppose you can have more than a crust of bread and gruel for dinner tonight. Maybe two crusts." Melody winked and her laughter filled the diner.

"Knowing you, Melody, I bet you could even make that taste good," Bob butted in. "In fact, those cinnamon rolls are calling my name." He sniffed the air.

"Oh yeah, I don't want to stop you from your treats." Melody glanced at her watch. "Oh, and speaking of treats, the garden club is waiting for their turnovers. I gotta run. No rest for the weary," she said with a quick wave and then headed into the kitchen.

Near the counter, Charlotte also noticed her son and daughter-in-law, Bill and Anna, in line waiting to order.

Their backs were to the door. As usual, they looked as if they had just stepped out of *Town & Country* magazine—with the emphasis on "town." Anna's dark hair was styled in a fancy twist on the back of her head, and she wore a smart pink sweater and matching slacks.

Charlotte quickly approached and leaned in close to Anna's ear. "Whatever you order, I'll take two."

"Mother!" Anna turned and opened her arms and offered Charlotte a quick hug. "Were the cinnamon rolls calling your name too?"

"Yes, well . . . since we were in town." Charlotte glanced back at Bob.

"Oh, by the way, we stopped by the farm on the way in." Anna lowered her voice. "Bill wanted to see how things were turning out."

Charlotte clicked her tongue. "When the work is done, I'm determined to have a talk with those sons of mine. I know they just wanted to help, to watch out for their dad, but I'm not so sure they went about it the right way."

From the look on Anna's face, Charlotte could tell she didn't agree. But instead of arguing, Charlotte looked across the restaurant where her granddaughters were exiting the bathroom. They wore matching plaid skirts and bright red sweaters. *Like two little dolls.*

"Girls, did you see who's here?" Anna said. "Come and say hi to your grandma and grandpa."

Jennifer and Madison rushed forward and gave Charlotte and Bob a quick hug.

Bob stood less than four feet away from Bill, but neither said a word.

"Grandpa, we went by your house but you weren't there. We saw Uncle Pete and the big machines in the field."

"The big green combines were so cool." Jennifer said. "I—

"Girls, did you want a cinnamon roll?" Anna interrupted. "Come tell me what you want."

Bill and Anna ordered, then sat at one of the booths.

Charlotte pursed her lips, wishing she hadn't given her opinion to Anna. She was sure that as soon as they were out of earshot Anna would spill every word.

"Hi, Charlotte. Bob," said Melody's assistant, Ginny. Ginny's long reddish hair was tucked up in a hairnet, reminding Charlotte of that *I Love Lucy* episode where Lucille Ball and her friend Ethel work at the chocolate factory. The uncertain anxiety in Ginny's face also matched Lucy's. "What can I get you today?"

"I'll have a bear claw. *Rrrr*." Christopher declared, raising his curled fingers for Ginny to see.

"You're just getting one of those 'cause you like saying that," Emily commented. "You've never even tasted one of those before."

"And for you?" the young woman behind the counter turned her attention to Emily. "What are you having?" Ginny asked, smacking her gum as she talked.

"I'll take a whole-wheat carob chip cookie, and a grande double-shot mocha with whip, please."

Charlotte glanced at Emily, unsure if she'd heard her right. For someone who made sure everything she ate or drank was healthy, that sure was a loaded drink—all the sugar, caffeine, and even the fat in the milk . . .

"Emily, are you sure?" Charlotte asked.

"Yes, a mocha." Emily's jaw was set.

"Coffee? You drink that stuff?" Ashley wrinkled her nose. "I'll have the same, but leave out the coffee. Just make mine a hot chocolate."

Ginny cocked her eyebrow at Ashley. "And you think I'm going to serve you? I think you can make your own hot chocolate."

Ashley sighed and hurried behind the counter.

"Emily just drinks coffee because it makes her seem like a grown-up." Christopher leaned against the counter.

"Do not."

"Do too."

"Oh, hush up, squirt"

"You are what you say!" Christopher spouted.

"Kids, that's enough," Bob stated sharply. The kids shut their mouths, but the argument continued in their sideways glances and flaring nostrils.

Bob pointed to the young woman helping Ginny. Her nametag read *Serena*. She had a long, black braid with a bright red bow tying it off. She carried a tray with a large bear claw on a plate.

"Christopher, I think that one's for you." Bob pointed to the plate.

Christopher's eyes widened as she handed him a pastry bigger than his two hands. "Cool."

A minute later Ginny handed Emily her cookie and coffee. After everyone had received their items, Bob stepped forward to the register to pay.

With quick fingers, red-bowed Serena punched the buttons on the old-fashioned register. "Okay, that's $20.25," she said with a grin.

Bob cleared his throat. "I don't think so, young lady. You must have pushed the wrong button."

She pulled the tape from the register, reading it over. "No, I got it right. Three sodas, $1.25 each. The two cinnamon rolls and bear claw are $2.50 each. The two cookies, $1.25. Hot chocolate $2.00, and mocha $4.50."

Bob's jaw dropped. "Did you say $4.50 for *coffee*? You've got to be kidding. That's highway robbery. How could it cost so much for coffee, sugar, and cream?"

The young woman pressed a hand onto her hip. "Yeah, well, $4.50 is the going rate. It's not just coffee. It's like a cappuccino with steamed milk . . ." She blabbered on, and Charlotte could tell it wasn't helping.

Reluctantly Bob pulled a $20.00 from his wallet and fished a quarter out of his front pocket. "Four fifty for coffee—" he muttered again under his breath.

Charlotte heard the slightest sniff and turned toward Emily. All the color had drained from their granddaughter's face. Without a word, Emily stepped forward and placed the coffee on the counter. Then with quick steps she hurried out the door and down the sidewalk, leaving the jingling of the three tiny bells on the glass door in her wake.

CHARLOTTE HURRIED DOWN Lincoln Street and noticed the leaves on the trees were already previewing their fall colors. Flags hung motionless from poles, their limp displays mimicking Charlotte's sinking heart.

She crossed the street and then paused before Fabrics and Fun, hoping Emily had stopped in to see Bob's sister, Rosemary. Looking through the window, she saw Rosemary standing near one of the first rows of colorful bolts. Her glasses, hanging from a gold chain around her neck, swung as she pointed out the newest fabrics to Celia Potts, one of the ladies from Charlotte's Bible study. Neither noticed Charlotte standing outside the window giving the store a quick scan. Emily wasn't anywhere in sight.

As she passed each business, she peered through the windows for any sign of Emily. She looked for the blonde hair and red sweatshirt. She also thought about what to say.

She considered defending Bob—explaining to Emily that her grandpa wasn't having the best of days. She thought about explaining Pete's decision to hire the combine team and how hard that was. She also thought about explaining to Emily that $4.50 for coffee really wasn't acceptable and that they needed to stick to a tight budget.

In the end, Charlotte considered what Denise would do. She hadn't been around her daughter very often to watch Denise in her role as mom. Still, the words her daughter had spoken to her years ago, before she ran away, replayed in her mind.

"Mom, you always have an explanation. You always have a lecture, but you never listen. You never take time to hear my side of things." Denise had said those words more than once. Charlotte had thought she'd listened, but looking back she realized most of the time she'd been too impatient. Being on the farm meant work. Hard work. There wasn't much time just to sit and shoot the breeze. Besides, Denise had been a girl. What had she known about life?

Charlotte crossed her arms and hugged them to herself more tightly. She imagined Emily did have a side—did have a reason for her reaction. The emotional retreat, mixed with

Emily's words last night about "not having anything to stick around for" told Charlotte there was something happening inside the girl's mind and heart. More than she let on.

Charlotte passed the remaining small shops and found herself at the end of Lincoln Street. There she looked across the street to the park and saw Emily sitting on a park bench. The bench was facing away from Charlotte, but she could tell from the slight shaking of the young girl's shoulders that the tears hadn't stopped.

Charlotte waited until an old truck passed, then walked across the street. She sat next to Emily without a word. Instead she just wrapped an arm around Emily's shoulders. The girl sat stiff and straight.

Emily pressed her lips together and tried to control her tears. Her attempts to hold back caused little bursts of emotion to break through in pitiful squeaks. After a minute, Emily crumbled. She pulled her thin legs up on the bench and leaned her cheek against Charlotte's shoulder.

"I'm sorry, Grandma. I didn't think the coffee was that much. I just—I just—"

Charlotte opened her mouth to speak, then remembered Denise's words and closed it again. "Um-hum."

After a minute passed, Emily took a deep, shuddering breath. "My mom and me . . . we liked to go to our favorite coffee shop. We'd always order the same thing. We both got a mocha and she—she—she'd call it our girl time."

"Sounds as if it was your special thing you did together." Charlotte tilted her head so she could see Emily's face. Her own fingers trembled slightly as she brushed the girl's bangs back from her forehead.

"Yeah, and it was during coffee time we'd work on our lists."

"Your lists?"

"You know, the list of five. Five places you'd like to visit someday, five favorite foods, five favorite movies."

Charlotte's heartbeat quickened. Her throat grew hot and thick. She closed her eyes and lifted her face to the sun, thinking about another young woman with her head on her shoulder. Without meaning to, a small squeak sounded from Charlotte's own lips as she tried to hold back her emotion.

"Listen to us. We sound like squeaky mice." Charlotte wiped a wayward tear.

Emily sat straight and turned to face her. "I'm sorry. I didn't mean to make you cry. I miss her, that's all—I'm sorry I brought it up."

"No, honey, don't be sorry. I'm glad you did. I never knew she did that with you. You see, your mom and I used to do the same thing, when she was your age."

"You did?"

Charlotte nodded. "Let me guess. Your mom's favorite movies were *Grease*, *The Sound of Music*, *The Princess Bride*, *It's a Wonderful Life*, and *Indiana Jones and the Temple of Doom*. I still don't know what she saw in that Indy movie."

"Yeah, those were her favorites! And when I mentioned I hadn't seen any of them we watched all five in one weekend."

Charlotte smiled, trying to imagine that.

"Actually, I think she thought that Indiana Jones guy was kinda cute," Emily confessed.

"And your mom's favorite foods?" Charlotte asked.

"Um, apple pie, tacos, asparagus, eggs Benedict, and chocolate."

"Apple pie?" Charlotte mouthed, remembering the apples she'd been peeling just this morning. She could make a pie instead of applesauce. A sad smile tugged at her lips, and she took Emily's hand. "I'm so glad you shared that. It makes me feel close to your mom again."

"I know. The thing I'm scared most of is that I'll forget what she looked like. How she laughed at the same jokes Christopher told over and over. How she'd poke Sam in the belly and tell him to stop growing. I especially never want to forget our coffee time."

"Let's work together and share more of our memories, often, to make sure that doesn't happen. We'll make sure neither one of us forgets, deal?"

"Deal." Emily patted Charlotte's hand. It wasn't a huge embrace, but it was a good start.

Someone cleared his throat behind them. She turned and noticed Bob standing there. The cup of frou-frou coffee seemed out of place in his large calloused hand.

"I thought you'd be in this direction. Expected you might want this too." Bob stretched out the coffee to Emily. She hesitated before taking it.

"Go ahead. I sure don't care to drink it. Your grandma would tan me if I even took a sip, especially seeing that I plan on eating half this cinnamon roll." He held up a small paper bag in his other hand.

"Thank you, Grandpa," Emily said, taking the coffee.

"Oh, and I guess there's a special deal," Bob slipped a small card out of his front shirt pocket. "That girl in there said that if I buy ten coffees I'd earn two for free." He paused and handed a card to Emily.

Charlotte's heart grew warm and a soft sigh escaped her lips.

"Really?" Emily took it and turned to Charlotte. "So, like, maybe we can come in sometime and have coffee? And talk?"

"I'd love to. I might even try that fancy coffee, though I'm more of a black-coffee girl myself."

They rose and turned back to the main street. A peaceful expression replaced Emily's tear-filled face of just moments before.

"Don't lose that card, you hear?" Bob mumbled.

Emily offered her grandpa a quick hug. And when she pulled back, he held on for just the briefest second.

He then turned to Charlotte and squeezed her shoulder. They watched Emily walk toward Ashley, who was waiting at the end of Lincoln Street. "Times change, don't they?"

"Yes, Bob Stevenson, that's right." Charlotte nodded. "But as long as we can share a cinnamon roll every once in a while I don't mind so much. Now show me what's hiding in that bag. And you better not have started in. Sometimes your half is more like three-fourths."

"And sometimes, woman, you pay *too* close attention to things . . ."

Chapter Twelve

Christopher thumbed through the pages of a thick book on spacecraft. The paper was glossy, and he noticed smudged fingerprints were left when he turned the page. He realized his fingers were still chocolately from the handful of chocolate chips he'd eaten. He had tried to save most of them for pancakes but couldn't help but eat a few.

He licked his fingers, then wiped them on the scratchy gray blanket and went back to his book. He was sure that somewhere he'd find a photo of a machine part similar to the rusty metal contraption he'd found in the field.

Sitting next to him was Fat Monkey, a new yard-sale find picked up by Uncle Pete. At first Grandma had insisted they wash the stuffed animal. But after Christopher showed her the tag still on it, she changed her mind. It was still like new, which meant it hadn't had a chance for "who knew what" to infest it.

He'd named it Fat Monkey because that was what it was. Black with a plastic face and a tuft of hair on the top of its head, the monkey had a stuffed belly that seemed too big for its body. Fat Monkey was big enough to hold in his hand or stuff into his backpack. It was the perfect pal to join him on his adventures and to look at books on spacecraft.

He picked up Fat Monkey and moved his face closer to the book to get a better view of the page that showed how rockets were built. Christopher studied the many parts.

"What do you think, Fat Monkey? Does it look anything like our contraption?"

Christopher wiggled his hand and Fat Monkey shook its head.

"No, I didn't think so either."

He heard footsteps downstairs and decided to check it out. They were heavy-booted footsteps—either Grandpa's or Uncle Pete's. Maybe they had chores to do. Maybe they needed his help.

Sometimes being around his grandparents and uncle was like finding out Santa Claus was real. He'd heard about them his whole life, but he couldn't remember ever seeing them, except in photos. They were different than the old neighbors in San Diego. Uncle Pete's and Grandpa's clothes were usually dirty. Their hands were big and rough. And they were more interesting than Santa—even without the presents.

He closed the book and jumped down from the bed, eager to see what man-work they needed help with.

Chapter Thirteen

Charlotte opened the barn door wide and let both light and fresh air flood into the space. As soon as they arrived home, Bob had hiked into the fields to check on the progress of the combine crews. He still didn't seem completely at peace with the decision, but he wasn't mad like he had been that morning.

Charlotte was happy about that. The harvest mattered, of course, and the income brought in by the crops was vital. But neither mattered as much as having her son and her husband get along. She needed them to help her with the kids, to help things run right around this place, not to cause more trouble.

Her feet crunched on the hay scattered on the ground, and she grabbed a feed bucket from the wall.

With Pete, Bob, and Sam in the fields, it looked as if the evening chores would be up to her. She thought about asking Emily and Christopher to help. But Christopher had been deep in a book, and Emily still seemed emotionally fragile from earlier that day. Add Charlotte's worry about the garden on top of all that, and her heart sank even deeper.

Charlotte fed the horses their oats and hay, pausing for just a moment to notice how strong and big Stormy looked already. The colt still watched her from a distance, peeking around Charlotte to see if anyone else—namely Emily—followed.

After Stormy's birth last spring, they'd all taken turns caring for the foal, but as the weeks and months passed it was Emily who gave Stormy the most attention, and Stormy made it clear she enjoyed Emily's company the best.

Stormy would dart around her mother with excitement every time Emily approached.

Charlotte fed the milk cows next and then made sure both the horses and the milk cows had enough water.

Her mind clicked through a list of things to finish before she headed back inside to start dinner. And she wondered if she'd have to make dinner for the whole crew. She'd picked up some extra chicken legs just in case. She also made a mental note to try to find Pete before she started cooking.

There were a thousand little things that always had to be done around the farm. Like weeds in a garden, they had to be taken care of. Over the years she had discovered that the more she let things slide, the worse the problem became.

"Like bats in the barn rafters," Charlotte mumbled to herself. "If I don't take care of them now, watch out."

Bats in the barn weren't unusual. Some people even found them in their attics. One or two bats didn't seem worth the fight, but today when she entered the barn, the odor of guano—bat waste—was strong. Bats, it seemed, were like rabbits when it came to reproducing. Two soon turned into too many.

She glanced at her watch, trying to estimate when the guys would be done in the fields. She thought about asking Pete to get rid of the bats, but he'd most likely be exhausted after a long day.

"There's no time like the present," she told herself. "Just do it and be done with it." It was something her mother had always said. Something she'd repeated with her own kids.

Charlotte's feet stirred dust as she walked across the straw. She grabbed the tall ladder and carried it outside. She leaned it against the side of the red planks and situated the dusty ladder so that the top shelf rested just below a round, open knothole.

Brushing her dirty hands on her jeans, she went back inside the barn and found a plastic, five-gallon bucket in the corner. She rinsed it out at the pump, and then she proceeded to fill it. As the water poured from the spigot, her mind again clicked through the things she had to do that evening: make dinner, finish making the apple pie, make sure the boys showered for church tomorrow, talk to Emily about her choices in clothes for church.

Charlotte smiled, and she realized she was learning. The more she prepped beforehand, the better. Even talking to the kids the night before about their attire helped. Not that they didn't still argue, but at least they had all night to work through the emotions instead of having the whole thing blow up right before they were due to head out the door.

When the water was only a few inches from the top of the five-gallon bucket, Charlotte lugged it over to the ladder.

This was the hard part—climbing with the bucket, balancing its weight, and setting it up on the top platform without incident.

"Okay, Lord, I know Your Word says that we can call on You as our strength, and I was wondering if that meant I can pray for help to make it to the top of this ladder." She moved the bucket from her right hand to her left, and stepped onto the first rung.

She was just about to try for the second when a familiar whistle caught her attention. She glanced to the side in time to notice Pete rounding the corner.

"I'll take the strong back on this young man as an answer to that prayer. Thank You, Lord."

Seeing her, Pete's eyes widened. "Need help with the bucket, Ma?" He hurried over and took the handle from her, and she stepped out of the way.

"You're back early. I didn't expect you until after dark."

"Yeah, well, it's amazing how fast things go with a whole team of men. And Sam was a big help today." He started up the ladder. "Bats nestling in again?"

"'Fraid so."

Within thirty seconds he had scaled to the top, set up the bucket, made sure it was secure, and climbed back down.

"That will show those bats." He glanced up at the bucket and nodded. "And speaking of critters, the coon was in the dry corn again. We're not going to have fuel for the corn burner if he keeps it up. That guy has made a mess of everything."

"Worse than your room?" Charlotte asked, leaning against the barn.

"My apartment," Pete corrected.

"Worse mess than your apartment?" Charlotte asked again.

"I'm not that bad." Pete smirked.

"Grandma?" Emily's voice carried from inside the barn.

"Out here!" Charlotte called, moving toward the front of the barn, following Emily's voice.

Emily rounded the corner before Charlotte got there. "Grandpa wanted to tell you that the oven is preheated for the pie."

"Good thing he sent you out. I forgot. You know how it takes forever for that thing to warm up. Maybe your grandpa will get me a new one someday." She smiled, realizing that Bob probably just hoped those peeled apples were for pie. She tucked her short, brown hair behind her ears.

Emily looked past Charlotte to the ladder and the bucket. "What's that?" Her brow furrowed.

"We're catching bats." Charlotte pointed up. "It's a trick Pete learned from one of his friends at the feed store."

"A trap? It doesn't look like a trap. How does it work?" Emily walked closer to the ladder, squinting to get a better look. She neared Charlotte, smelling of strawberry shampoo and wet nail polish. Emily had put her hair into two messy buns on the sides of her head, and her face was makeup free. Charlotte thought she looked cute like that—like a young girl should.

"See that open knothole?" Pete pointed to the spot just above the bucket. "When we lock up the barn tight for the night, the knothole is the bats' favorite way to exit."

"They can fit through that? It doesn't look very big."

"It's not," Pete commented. "Their bodies squeeze out of that hole, and the only way they can get airborne is to sweep down first. The water in that bucket catches them."

"Catches them?" Emily folded her arms over her chest and from the intense look Charlotte could tell she was trying to picture it.

"Yep, by tomorrow morning the bucket will be full." Pete grinned.

Charlotte turned to the house—to dinner and the pie.

"Then what?" Emily's words caused her to pause. "Do you take them somewhere to release them?"

Laughter burst from Pete's lips. "Hey, Mom, Miss Golden State wants to know where we release them. I'll tell you what, when their limp bodies—"

Charlotte slugged him hard in his arm. "Pete, have you no compassion? Give the girl a break." She turned her attention back to Emily.

The color was already draining from Emily's face.

"Actually, we, uh, don't release them, because they're not alive. I filled the bucket with water, Emily. They drown."

"You drown the poor little creatures?" Emily's voice rose in anger. Tears pooled in her eyes. "I've never heard anything so cruel in all my life." Her lower lip trembled.

"Honey, they carry disease and make a mess." Charlotte sighed. "People can get really sick from the guano. It can even make people lose their eyesight. Not to mention the smell and all their waste that we have to clean up. Unless you volunteer to do it. I can give you a bucket and a mop."

"I didn't say *that*, but they don't purposely live their lives trying to cause more work for you. They are just doing what God made them to do. That doesn't mean you have to *kill* them."

Pete leaned close. He spoke into Charlotte's ear, whispering loud enough for Emily to hear. "Wow, with that reaction, you definitely don't want to mention what happens to the coons."

Charlotte shot Pete the look—the same one she'd been giving him since he was three. A look that plainly declared he'd said enough.

"Coons? As in raccoons? Do you kill them *too*?" More tears pooled in Emily's lids.

As if finally realizing the impact of his words, Pete glanced toward Charlotte and then back to Emily. "Um . . . not always." His tone was softer. "Sometimes we *do* release them far from the farm. It's not that we want to hurt them or move them. We take care of our animals best by dealing with the pests."

One tear broke through and slid down Emily's freshly scrubbed cheek. Pete's look of amusement softened. His eyes darted to Charlotte's—he didn't know what to say.

Charlotte took a deep breath. The truth was she didn't always like how things worked, but her granddaughter needed to realize that she wasn't trying to be cruel. That's just how things happened on a farm. "Emily, the fact is—"

"The fact is," Pete interrupted. "I've been thinking about other ways." He glanced at his mom, seeking her approval. "I've been considering trying other things on this farm. New ideas."

He moved back to the ladder and glanced at Emily. "Are you interested in helping me figure out another way? I'll take this down for now, and if you think of something, we can try it. I can ask the guys at the feed store too. Maybe they have other ideas."

"You mean we can think of a way to capture them and release them without hurting them?" Emily approached and held the ladder as Pete scaled it. She smiled up at him. "I'm sure we can think of something, *farm boy*."

Pete grabbed the bucket and dumped it. It poured from the top of the ladder and splashed to the ground just a few feet from where Emily stood. She squealed and jumped back. Then he hurried back down the ladder with the empty bucket swinging in his hand. At the bottom rung he jumped to the ground and then handed her the bucket. "As you wish."

"Are you quoting from that movie again?" Charlotte glanced from one to the other, noting how similar their features were when they had silly grins on their faces.

"I don't know, are we, Buttercup?"

Emily smiled slightly and nodded.

"Actually, you look more like Princess Leia with your hair all done up on the sides like that."

"Princess who?"

"Princess Leia. You know, from *Star Wars*."

"Don't you mean Queen Amidala?"

"No, not those new ones. Those are totally *not* the real *Star Wars*. I'm talking about the real stuff."

Emily's eyebrows formed a V. "Oh, yeah, those people in those *old* movies. I didn't like them as much."

He glanced toward Charlotte. "What is it with kids these days? You'd think living so close to Hollywood they would have had a clue about the classics."

"Yes, well, I'll leave you two to this discussion. I'm gonna check on Grandpa. Leaving him alone in the kitchen with a full fridge and an empty stomach is a bad idea."

Pete chuckled his agreement, but his eyes stayed intent on Emily. She was starting to describe a few traps that might work without hurting the animals. They weren't practical or efficient, yet Pete listened, and he promised to try them next week.

"God bless him," Charlotte muttered as she hurried to the house. "Twice the work, half the results."

But deep inside she also had to admit she was pleased. Pete actually gave Emily the time of day instead of poking fun at her. He seemed to be enjoying his time with the kids more and more, and they liked him.

Life was changing around the farm. Things weren't going to continue on as they'd always been. For a long while, she, Bob, and Pete had been in a rut. It was a contented rut, but it was a rut all the same.

With everything in her, she wished for her daughter to still be alive—for her grandchildren to have their mother— but with God's help they were not only learning to adjust but also growing and changing too.

She walked up the steps and into the house, giving Toby a pat on the head as she passed. The dog wagged the brown and black plume of her tail. Inside, Charlotte scanned the kitchen, noting orange peels on the counter just a few feet from the trash. She heard a shower going in the upstairs bathroom and guessed it was Sam.

She sighed as she tossed the peels into the trash, and she knew that if she didn't have a real meal on the table quickly they'd *all* descend upon the kitchen and eat up the quick-and-easy food she'd bought for the school lunches.

She found herself humming "Awesome God," one of her favorite praise songs, as she made a flour mixture to use on the chicken before she fried it up. As a habit, she also got a veggie-burger patty out of the freezer to cook for Emily's dinner. The weird thing was, she could hardly remember what it was like not to have to think of a vegetarian alternative to go with their meals.

Before the accident, before the kids came, life on the farm had consumed her time and taxed her body. But now there were three new lives with their own special needs. Three kids who needed food, care, and training. Three kids who also needed moral and spiritual tending.

"Oh, Lord, give me the wisdom." She opened the fridge and squatted down to get a head of lettuce from the bottom drawer. A pain shot through her back as she rose, and she pressed her hand against her lower back as she placed the lettuce on the cutting board. "And the strength to do what I have to do."

The prayer hadn't completely passed her lips when Pete burst through the door and sauntered in. "Hey, Mom, I was thinking the kids could come over to my place tonight for a movie. You don't mind, do you?"

"Mind? Not really. In fact, it might be a nice break." The words were barely out of her mouth when she remembered how mad Bob had been earlier that day.

"Actually, Emily and Christopher can, but not Sam. He needs to finish his homework—or rather, *start* it."

"Homework? Can't that wait?" Pete pushed his hands deeper into his jeans pockets. "He's been working hard all day—"

"No, it can't." Charlotte shot him a hard gaze.

He leaned back. "Fine. Sam can come another day." And with that he slumped down in the dining room chair with his brow furrowed, as if worried she was going to make *him* help Sam with his homework.

A few minutes later, the pitter-patter of Christopher's feet coming down the stairs met Charlotte's ears.

"Okay, Uncle Pete, my room is clean. I took a shower. I'm ready to watch the *Star Wars* movie."

Pete rose, grabbed an apple from the counter, and headed out the door with Christopher hot on his heels.

"Hey, do you want me to make you a few plates when dinner's done?" Charlotte called to them. "I can have Emily bring it up later."

"Nah, Emily's already up there. She's 'airing out' my place."

"She says it smells like dirty socks," Christopher said.

"We'll grab some chicken after the movie. Save us some." Pete stepped back inside the door, reached into the pantry, and tucked a box of crackers under his arm.

"Yeah, after the movie." Christopher hurried away with a wave.

"Well, I'll be. Sometimes help comes in mysterious ways," Charlotte mumbled to herself as she checked on the chicken.

Chapter
Fourteen

Christopher didn't know what to expect when he turned the knob and opened the door to Uncle Pete's apartment. It was bright inside, mostly because there were three large windows that overlooked the farm.

"Whoa." Christopher walked to the window, noticing that he could see the road, the barn, and even Grandma talking on the phone in the kitchen.

He sniffed but didn't smell anything weird. He didn't think it smelled like dirty socks—more like buttered popcorn.

The walls were weird. They had big pink flowers on them that looked like they'd been there a long time because some of the flowers had lost their color and were almost white.

There was a big kitchen, almost as big as Grandma's kitchen. There was a couch by the windows and a big TV that looked a lot newer than Grandpa's TV.

Emily was in the living room tossing all sorts of socks into a pile with two fingers. With her other hand she pinched her nose. Christopher's jaw dropped open. He'd never seen so many dirty socks in his life. There had to be fifty of them.

Emily unpinched her nose. "Gee, Uncle Pete. Don't you ever do your laundry?"

Christopher turned around and saw Uncle Pete shrug.

"It's easier to just buy new socks. What's it to you?" Pete offered a fake scowl.

Emily rolled her eyes, then she stomped into the kitchen and took a six-pack of root beer out of a plastic bag. She then stomped back to the pile and filled the plastic bag with the socks.

"I'll be back. I'm going to go throw these in the washer." She pointed a finger at her uncle's chest. "Don't start the movie without me."

Emily hurried out the door and jogged down the steps.

Pete placed his hands on his hips and fluttered his eyelashes. He spoke in a high-pitched voice. "Girls . . . they are so picky!"

Christopher laughed so hard that he got a stitch in his side. Uncle Pete pranced to the green couch and then swept kernels of popcorn off the cushions with his hand and settled down onto the sagging seat.

Christopher sniffed the air. "It smells like popcorn *and* dirty socks." He walked a slow circle, glancing at the odd room. There were photos hanging on the walls of pretty flowers and sunrises. But on top of a cabinet were all types of tools—screwdrivers, scissors, pliers, as if Uncle Pete had just found them in his pocket at the end of the day and tossed them there.

Pete flipped on the television, and previews of other movies began to play. Two guys were talking on the preview and said a kinda-bad word. Then they did something funny that made Pete laugh. Christopher looked at him, and Uncle Pete, as if just remembering that Christopher was there, turned down the volume.

Christopher nodded his approval, then pointed up at a buck mounted on the wall. "Is that thing real?"

"Are you asking if it's a real deer? It used to be. That's Betty. I got it my first time hunting."

Christopher took a step closer. "Are her eyes real?"

"Actually, it was a buck. A boy deer. Not a she. And no, the eyes are glass." Pete chuckled. "Emily hates that thing."

Christopher didn't want to know how the head got from the deer to being put on that wood. He took a step back and glanced at Uncle Pete.

"So if it's a boy, why did you give him a girl's name?" Christopher settled into one of the couch's cushy corners.

"It started one night when I was out with my friends. We were, uh, out playing pool, you know, just hanging out, and there was this girl who wouldn't leave me alone."

"A girl?"

"Well, a woman actually."

"Was she pretty?"

"Sort of, but that's not the point."

"What is the point?"

"The point is that she wasn't my type, and I can't believe I'm having this conversation with a ten-year-old."

"Ten and a half. I'll be eleven in April."

"Anyway, back to Betty, I told this woman that I couldn't be her, uh, friend because I had Betty waiting at home."

"And she didn't know it was a deer?"

"Nope, and in order for me not to lie, I named her Betty."

"Yeah, lying isn't good." Christopher smiled, realizing Uncle Pete's explanation made complete sense. But . . . he looked around again. "I still don't get it. Why do you have all the flowers and stuff around? Maybe for a wife some-day? Girls like flowers."

Uncle Pete laughed. His laugh was big and loud.

"I thought you knew. This place used to be where my grandma lived—your great-grandma. We built this apart-ment for her when my parents took over the main house." Pete looked around the room. "The wallpaper, the flower pictures, and the couch—it was just her stuff. When I first moved in here after she died, I thought I'd change things." He shrugged. "But there's no need really, it's just me."

The door opened and Emily entered. Christopher pressed his lips together.

Uncle Pete patted the cushion next to him. "Hey, thanks for washing my socks, Em. You ready for the movie?"

She rolled her eyes and walked to the kitchen. "I'm thirsty. Do you have any glasses for ice?" She opened a cabinet and paused. "Uncle Pete, what is this?"

Christopher hurried over and noticed that the cabinet wasn't filled with dishes. It had trophies, a couple of books, and some framed photographs.

"Hey, that's my stuff," Pete yelled.

Emily pulled out a photograph and pressed it to her chest. "I wasn't snooping. I was just looking for a glass."

Pete moved toward her, and Emily took a quick look at the photograph before he got there.

"No way, Uncle Pete . . . this is Miss Simons—Sam's English teacher. When was this taken, like twenty years ago?"

"Only fifteen years. At our junior prom." He reached for the photograph. "Give me that."

Emily took a closer look at the photograph. "Man, Uncle Pete, you were skinny . . . and your hair was puffy." She cocked her head. "Miss Simons was pretty, though—even with poodle hair."

"It was the style back then." He took the photograph from her and put it back in the cupboard. "Glasses are in the other shelf—to the right of the sink."

Emily took a glass out and filled it up with tap water. "You should ask her out again. You're a young, handsome bachelor. You really shouldn't be spending your weekends entertaining us."

Christopher poked Uncle Pete's shoulder. "Yeah. Miss Simons is pretty. Is she your type?"

"Of course she's his type. Why wouldn't she be?" Emily leaned forward, her eyes wide. "And when did you consider who was Uncle Pete's type or not? You don't even know what that means."

Christopher pressed his lips together again.

Uncle Pete grabbed the remote. "Okay, I'll keep that in mind."

Christopher scrunched his nose and sighed. "Can we watch the movie now?"

"Good idea," Uncle Pete said.

They moved back to the living room and found their seats.

Christopher looked toward Uncle Pete, and Uncle Pete unpaused the movie. "This is going to be good."

Thankfully, Emily nodded and turned her attention to the TV. "Yeah, it might be good, but nothing's as good as *The Princess Bride*, right?"

"Right, Buttercup," Uncle Pete said with a chuckle.

"Can you turn it up?" Emily asked as the movie started.

Pete pushed the button until the volume rose so loud that the windows quivered. Then Uncle Pete said something. Christopher wasn't sure what it was, but it sort of sounded like, "As you wish."

Chapter
Fifteen

The smell of percolating coffee wafted through the house. Charlotte could make out the sound of Bob humming "Amazing Grace" as he shaved. Bob always hummed hymns on Sundays.

Charlotte yawned, anticipating her first cup of coffee. She needed it this morning. Needed something to pull her out of the murky fog filling her mind.

She headed to the kitchen, realizing that last night she hadn't ironed a skirt for church like she'd planned to. After dinner and Bob's Bible reading, Emily and Christopher had come back to the house long enough to grab some chicken and long enough for Christopher to announce that he was changing Fat Monkey's name to Chewbacca, like the furry creature in *Star Wars*.

After dinner, Sam had sat in the dining room, spending more energy looking dejected than doing his homework.

"You can lead a kid to his books, but you can't make him work," Bob had mumbled as they headed to bed.

And somewhere in the middle of all the drama she'd forgotten about her ironing. Now she'd have to hurry if they were to make it to church on time.

A few minutes later, the ironing board was set up.

She lifted the hot iron and smoothed it over the skirt, enjoying the way the wrinkles disappeared with each pass. She heard the groan of the hot water heater and the sound of the shower upstairs. It had to be Emily, and her guess was that Christopher was already out with his Uncle Pete, feeding the animals. The younger two had learned early on that life was better if Grandma *didn't* have to pound on their bedroom doors over and over to wake them up. Of course, Sam wasn't as easy. He still didn't rouse until she'd knocked on his door numerous times.

She glanced at the clock on the wall, telling herself she'd start her pounding when the shower stopped. No matter if she started an hour ahead of time or fifteen minutes, each time she told Sam to get up he always told her he would. But the truth was he usually didn't get up until he smelled bacon frying or noted the scents of other breakfast offerings.

"Today, he'll be lucky for a bowl of cereal," Charlotte muttered as she set down the iron. She readjusted the skirt and then began to iron it again. "I'm not going to play his game any longer. If he isn't at the table when the food is placed there, he can find his own breakfast."

She pressed the hot iron over the cotton, wishing she could as easily press the worries out of her mind.

It wasn't one thing that weighed on her mind, but a thousand little worries. Just what was Christopher hiding? Would Sam pass English? What if he didn't? What if he turned out like Pete? And what about the garden—what or who had gotten into it? And would they be back?

Like marbles filling up a jar, each one wasn't much to be

concerned about, but when they were stacked altogether there was little breathing space among them.

It had started when she'd been awakened by a bad dream. In it Denise was a teenager again, sneaking out and hanging with the wrong crowd. Charlotte had tried to find her to talk some sense into her, but Denise wasn't to be found.

Charlotte woke up, frantic, and then reminded herself that it was only a dream. She'd fallen back asleep only to have another one in which Christopher was lost. Again, she looked and looked, but she couldn't find him. Worried, she went over to the grain truck, and she found his tennis shoes in the grain bin. Thankfully, she'd awakened before that dream unfolded.

And despite eight hours of sleep, in the morning her limbs felt heavy and her energy was gone. The thought of cooking breakfast, getting ready for church, and having to put on a happy face in front of her friends added more marbles to her worry jar.

But, as she'd done through many seasons of change on the farm, Charlotte knew she would do what she had to do. She'd put one foot in front of another.

She finished ironing the skirt and shook it out, laying it over the ironing board. She took a mug from the yellow cupboard, noting like she often did as of late that the cabinets could use a fresh coat of paint. In fact, all the cupboards were chipped on the corners. Maybe she and Emily could tackle that project once harvest was over.

She lifted the coffeepot to pour herself a cup just as Christopher's voice pierced the air. "Grandma, Grandma, Grandma!"

The door opened, and she heard the screen door slam shut. "It's happened again. They came back!"

"Who came back?" She glanced out the window, not seeing any new cars in the driveway.

"The people or..." Christopher's face scrunched as he paused. "Or the things who messed up the garden."

"You're kidding." Charlotte set the mug on the counter.

"No, I'm not. Come on. I'll show you."

Christopher took her hand and tugged. Charlotte paused to slip on her shoes and then followed.

They rounded the corner of the house to spy the garden, and Charlotte let out a low moan. The row of green peppers she'd left to grow a little bigger in the warmth of the Indian summer was gone.

Just yesterday, large green zucchinis had nestled under the green stalks like oversized jellybeans that had escaped from the vending machine near the front door of Mel's Place. Today only two scrawny zucchinis remained.

Not only that, the bean plants looked as if they'd been shredded by a weed eater, with torn leaves scattered everywhere.

She squatted and lifted a handful of dark, rich soil, letting it sift through her fingers. "Who, or what, could have done this?"

"I think that's what Toby's trying to find out."

Toby trotted through the garden, scurrying over the already trampled ground. She sniffed the ground, and her tail drooped as if she was unhappy with the scent.

"What do you smell, Toby? Huh, girl?" Christopher asked.

Charlotte stood and brushed the dirt from her hands. "I

wish she could tell us. It would really be great if I could talk 'dog' right now."

Charlotte walked around the edge of the garden. She thought she spotted some boot prints, but she couldn't be sure if they'd been there before and she just hadn't noticed them. "Christopher, can you go get Pete?"

"I already did. He saw it first."

"Really? What did he say?" Charlotte glanced around, wondering where he could have disappeared to.

"He's showering for church. He said something about maybe seeing an old friend there."

"Church? Pete's going to church?" The words blurted from her lips, but as Christopher looked up at her she tried to hide her surprise. Pete hadn't been a regular church attendee for many years.

A memory drifted back—that of Dana and Pete sitting side by side at church as teens. Had he run into her? Talked to her? A spot of hope brightened Charlotte's heart.

"Okay, but what did he say about the garden? Are these footprints?"

Christopher shrugged. "Uncle Pete can't tell if they're from us or someone else. He said with all the extra people around that it's hard to figure out what ones don't belong. He thinks it's animals."

"Animals? Like coons?" She remembered the conversation from yesterday. But surely coons couldn't carry away medium-sized zucchinis, could they?

"Somethin' like that." Christopher gave a sharp whistle, and Toby trotted over.

Charlotte placed her hands on her hips. In all the years she'd had a garden, she'd seen nothing like this. "It's a mystery, for sure. One that needs to be figured out." She glanced at her watch. "But now's not the time to think about this. Time to head to church, mister."

Forty minutes later they were pulling out in Bob's truck with stomachs full of cold cereal and toast. Bob didn't have the happiest of looks on his face, and Charlotte hoped not too many fellow parishioners would ask him about the harvest and how things were turning out. Was it bad to pray that everyone would be unfriendly today?

Fifteen minutes later, their truck crested the small hill on which Bedford Community Church was located. The white church appeared like any other that dotted the countryside, with front steps leading up to wide doors and a steeple pointed straight to heaven. But this was not just any church. This was *her* church—filled with people she'd known all her life. They'd walked beside her through the good times and the challenging ones. The hard thing was that on days like today they'd not only welcome her in but also see the truth behind her smile. There was no pretending with these folks.

Bob parked in the gravel parking lot, and Charlotte noticed Dana's small, red hatchback a few cars down. Charlotte hadn't asked Pete about it, but he'd looked especially spit-and-shined as he'd climbed into his old truck this morning. He'd left a few minutes before them, and Lazarus was parked under the oak tree.

"Pete must already be inside," she mumbled to no one in particular.

They climbed out of the truck, a look of resignation on Sam's face. Emily didn't look as glum as she had during the prior Sundays. To her, attending church had become another opportunity to see Ashley and possibly help in the church nursery. Maybe attending youth group had also helped warm Emily to being there. Charlotte hoped it did. She hoped nice friends would draw Emily into the one place where she could learn about the greatest Friend of all.

Christopher's nose was in another one of those books. This one was on outer space.

Chewbacca sat on the seat next to him. Christopher didn't seem in a hurry to budge, or to have even noticed they were at their destination. He seemed to be studying a drawing of a spacecraft and his eyes held a far-off look.

As he ate his cereal that morning, Christopher had hinted more than once that a telescope would be a great thing to have. As she opened his side door, Charlotte made a mental note to make sure the screens on Christopher's windows were locked tight to discourage any rooftop stargazing.

"Christopher, you'd better leave that book and that animal in the car."

He nodded but kept reading. It was only after Bob walked around the vehicle, cleared his throat, and placed a hand on Christopher's shoulder that the cropped-haired boy placed the book on the seat, making a tent over Chewbacca to keep it open to the right spot. Then he jumped down to the ground and slammed the door.

They approached to the sound of organ music, which Mary Henner always played to welcome members in, and to remind them it was time to stop visiting and to find their seats. Inside the foyer, Charlotte was surprised to find Pete waiting for them, arms crossed over a dress shirt that she hadn't seen him wear since Bill's younger daughter Jennifer's baby dedication.

Pete shifted his weight from side to side, glancing between the sanctuary and the front door, as if trying to decide whether to go in or to bolt. His eyes widened as he saw Charlotte, as if thankful for this distraction.

"So did Christopher show you the garden?" His voice had a nervous twinge to it and his normally playful grin had been replaced by thin, drawn lips. He ran his fingers through his hair, combing it back and patting it into place even though it looked perfectly fine. He might be asking about the garden, but Charlotte could tell that was the smallest worry on his mind.

"Yes, but shouldn't we talk about that after church?" Charlotte whispered. She motioned for Bob and the kids to go on ahead. Bob nodded and then pointed to the kids to head in before him. They shuffled forward in a single line with as much enthusiasm as cattle lining up to get branded.

"Yeah, I suppose, unless they need help in the nursery." Pete ran his hands down the seams of his pants, and then crossed his arms over his chest as if trying to figure out what to do with his fidgeting hands.

"Nursery?"

Pete's eyes darted to the sanctuary again. In the third row from the front on the left side sat Dana Simons.

"Oh, now I get it. Pete, it's just Dana. She's a sweet girl . . . she doesn't bite."

"Yeah, but she's sitting in *our* seat."

"Our name isn't on it."

Besides it's not like you've sat in the pew in a while, she wanted to add.

"But she knows that's our row."

Dana glanced over her shoulder, brushing her dark hair from her face, watching Bob and the kids approach. She smiled and scooted closer to the far end of the pew to make room for them all.

"She has the right to sit anywhere she wants. Besides, it was the row she was used to sitting in too, before . . ."

Charlotte watched as Sam arrived at the pew first. He paused, realizing his teacher was sitting in the row, and motioned for Christopher to go ahead of him. Christopher sat by Dana. Then Sam, then Emily, then Bob. The worship leader approached the front and the first worship song began.

"See, there's nothing to be afraid of. There will be five people separating the two of you."

"Yeah, but why do you think she's here?" Pete asked.

"My guess is she's here to worship God, and my suggestion is that you get your heart and mind focused to do the same."

Pete shrugged, and then motioned Charlotte forward. She entered, made her way to the third row, and sat. Pete sat beside her, his fingers tapping against his legs. Charlotte patted his hand.

They sang a few more songs, greeted each other, listened to an announcement, and then Pastor Nathan Evans got up to preach. She guessed it to be a good sermon, but it was only as she got up to leave that Charlotte realized she couldn't remember a word of it. Instead, her mind had been on everything else *but* the sermon. On the harvest, on coffee time with Emily, on Pete and Dana and small hopes for the two of them, on Sam's report that he still hadn't started, and on Christopher's discovery that morning.

An unsettled stirring in her gut made it hard to get her mind off the farm. There were changes. Many could be expected, but some made no sense.

As the congregation rose to sing a closing song, Charlotte was determined to get to the bottom of things. She couldn't control the people around her, but she could figure out what, or who, was getting into her carrots.

THE CASE OF THE MISSING VEGETABLES had everyone's attention at lunch.

"I'm gonna set up some traps to capture any critters." Pete took a large bite of his sandwich.

Emily's eyes widened.

"Just to capture 'em, not to kill 'em," he quickly added, speaking out of the side of his mouth as he chewed.

"What about a stakeout?" Emily lifted an eyebrow and her blue-shadowed eyes widened. "Sam, Christopher, and I can sleep in the barn tonight. We'll take our sleeping bags and stuff, and . . ."

Charlotte swallowed her bite of ham sandwich. "I don't think so. You have school tomorrow. And if there *is* something out there, that would be far too dangerous." A sinking feeling expanded in her chest as she said those words. It was as if speaking of the danger made it real to her.

Too dangerous? She put her sandwich on her plate, suddenly not hungry. In all the years she'd lived on Heather Creek Farm—since she was a young bride—she'd never felt unsafe. The only time they locked their doors was when they were going to Harding for the day. And they almost never locked them at night. If she were to guess, she would say it was some*one* rather than some*thing*. Animals were random. They left evidence of their eating frenzy behind. They left half-eaten vegetables and often dug holes—neither of which had happened in her garden.

"I think Pete's idea is fine. Traps are good. I'm sure he can make one that won't harm the creatures," she added for emphasis. "The barn just isn't safe."

"Nonsense," Bob piped up from his seat at the head of the table. "I slept in that barn half my growin' up years—school or no school."

Charlotte stared at him, unsure if she'd heard him correctly. He continued eating as if his words were no big deal. As if he was telling the kids they could have an extra cookie after lunch instead of agreeing that it was perfectly fine to have a sleepover in the barn, on a school night, with something dangerous prowling around.

Charlotte's appetite completely vanished. She rose and began clearing off the table. She was screwing the lid on the jar of mayonnaise when Bob approached, taking the jar from her hand.

"I think the kids can finish this up." He spoke with a loud, authoritative tone as if letting the kids know he was giving an order, not merely making a suggestion. "Why don't we take a walk down to the creek?"

Charlotte glanced into his face, seeing a peace there she

hadn't witnessed in months. Viewing the serenity in his gaze brought on conflicting emotions—stirrings of both envy and curiosity.

She glanced at the mess in the kitchen and thought of the pile of laundry waiting, but when she looked again at Bob, she noted a plea in his eyes that she couldn't refuse.

She walked toward the back door and took her sweater off the hook. "Sure. I'd love to."

Chapter
Sixteen

Charlotte strolled beside Bob, each step bringing more questions about the purpose of their walk. She tried to push her worry and her to-do list out of her mind. Those things would always be there. This moment shouldn't be missed.

They used to go for walks all the time, especially before they had kids. After the kids were grown they'd started up again, but they hadn't walked in many months. Charlotte rubbed her thumb against Bob's, considering that perhaps this was a sign that things were starting to return to normal.

They walked hand-in-hand down the narrow dirt path toward the creek. It seemed strange not to have Toby by her side, but the dog had chosen to stay back with Christopher.

She glanced around, taking in the expansive sky and the land that stretched fertile and flat in every direction. From the house, one would never guess the creek was even there. It didn't appear to be more than a line of trees that ran through the pasture where the cows grazed. Yet it was an oasis of sorts, a place of calm in the midst of a busy farm.

Over the years she'd walked this path more times than she could count. As a new wife, she'd walked down to the creek to read her Bible, to pray, or to pace and toss rocks and let out steam after she discovered the perfect man she married wasn't nearly as perfect as she'd thought.

The wind picked up, carrying a scent of sunshine and prairie grass. It whipped her hair into her face and pressed against her back as if urging her forward.

She'd often carried her babies to the creek's banks for a breath of fresh air. Bill had taken his first steps trying to catch a bird that had hopped along the shoreline. Denise had taken off swimming like a fish in the creek's fresh waters when she was only three. And Pete had been the one who'd always come home with a water snake, frog, or even a fish he'd found in the shallows.

The path moved through the trees, then the clearing opened and the creek made a lazy loop. It flowed south, heading off into the distance. But for a moment, the bluish green water was here, and it was theirs.

In the branches overhead, the wind gentled to a whisper. Bob scanned the sky. He looked to the north, then to the south, reading it for any signs of a storm.

"Is it gonna rain?" Charlotte lowered herself onto the grassy bank.

"Nah, at least not in the next thirty minutes. But who knows? Our weather changes in the flick of a cow's tail." It was a saying Bob had come up with years ago, and it was one of his favorites.

A bird called in a nearby tree, and Charlotte glanced up at the branches, searching for a nest. She noted that a few green leaves had already started turning to straw-bale yellow.

"Remember when I found that arrowhead here?" Bob's words held a hint of longing for times past.

"Yes, I do." Charlotte squeezed Bob's hand. "It was on the day you proposed. Right after, in fact. You told me that you'd lived on this creek your whole life and had never found one. You told me that Cupid struck for sure."

"I still have that arrowhead. It's in the top drawer of my dresser."

"Really?" Charlotte felt heat rising to her cheeks, and she guessed those words gave her the same warm feelings as flowers and chocolate gave to most women.

He shrugged. "Yep, along with my dozen pairs of brand-new work gloves. It seems like I get a new pair every Christmas." He bent over, picked up a stone, and then plunked it into the creek. "Not that I'll get a chance to ever use them all."

The romantic feelings fled, and Charlotte wondered if she'd just imagined the earlier peace in his gaze. Perhaps she was mistaken and it was just plain weariness.

"Is there a reason you've taken me on a walk? Something you need to tell me? Or did you just need a few minutes to vent?" She kicked at a dirt clod, wondering if she could hold back her worry that simmered. She could be strong for just so long, and she wasn't sure she could help carry anyone else's burdens at this moment.

"Just thought you needed some fresh air."

"Fresh air? I need to catch up on the laundry before school tomorrow. And then check to see if the kids have any homework. You know how they always leave it for Sunday night."

"Maybe they'll learn a lesson then."

He tugged her hand and led her down the creek in the direction of Hannah's house. They used to joke that if Charlotte ever got tired of walking she could always float an inner tube down for a visit.

They walked for a few more minutes, and Charlotte willed herself to relax, to take in the sweet air of September. To enjoy this moment without replaying yesterday's concerns or trying to figure out which ones might show up next week.

"You know, what Pastor Evans said today made sense." Bob glanced at her.

Charlotte pressed her lips together, trying to remember just what the pastor had talked about. It was something about the fruit of the Spirit. But she was ashamed to admit she'd spent more time jotting down a grocery list of things she'd forgotten on yesterday's visit to the store than jotting down the Scripture references the pastor had shared.

"Um-hum," she said, hoping Bob would expound on his thoughts.

"I especially liked what he said about kindness. Jesus trained them and sent them out. He helped them to understand, but also made them stand on their own two feet. It's reaching down to help someone, but not doing everything for them."

Charlotte kept quiet, waiting for him to continue. It wasn't typical for Bob to talk like this, to share his heart, and she didn't want her babbling to get in the way.

"I never thought of it like that, but it makes sense," Bob added.

As he strolled, Bob reached down and plucked a strand of prairie grass, twirling it between his fingers.

"Hmm." Charlotte nodded. "I never had either. I mostly thought of kindness as doing for someone."

"That's why I felt it was okay for the kids to sleep in the barn tonight. They need to toughen up. We've almost been apologetic about what this farm is. They're going to be here a while. They're not outsiders looking in."

"I never thought of it like that, but I suppose you're right." Charlotte sighed. "I guess I've been so busy trying to match what they had—in small ways—that I forget our place has something worthy to offer." She let her eyes rest on the cool blue water. "Things are different here, but in a good way. It's been a good place to share a life, Bob. A good life."

She looked at him and saw a slight smile. They continued on, neither saying much. A few white daisies danced and nodded in the breeze, bidding greetings as they passed on the footpath. Seeing the wildflowers reminded Charlotte of something Bob had told her long ago. It had been after Denise had run away, and they'd spent many dark nights worrying about her and many long days praying and calling any service organizations they could think of in San Diego. Anyone who might be able to keep an eye out for a pregnant girl and her boyfriend.

Charlotte had needed Bob then. Needed his words of assurance that God was watching over Denise, needed his prayers. Instead, there'd been many times when Bob just disappeared. He'd headed off somewhere on the farm, forcing her to answer the returned calls, and leaving her to retell the pitiful story alone to a person on the other end of the line who'd most likely heard similar stories a dozen times a day.

After confessing her frustration one stormy night, Bob

had made a confession of his own. He'd told her that he felt closest to God in nature, and that he saw sermons in the wildflowers. He wasn't leaving to get away from her, but to get to God.

For many years she had no idea what "sermons in the wildflowers" meant, but seeing the white daisies blooming now, long past time for summer flowers, reminded her of what she had discovered. Nature had its own way, its own surprises.

Instead, why did she try so hard to make everything fit her system? She was the type of person who always wanted everything planned out, to make things work in the right order at the right time. But maybe there could be joy in surprises and in change.

For the past few months she'd asked God over and over how he could have taken away these children's mother. Charlotte had lamented about all they'd lost. And now, she realized, maybe she should consider all they'd gained too. A beautiful home. Caring, male role models, which was something they'd never had. The chance to know their extended family, their roots. A chance to learn new skills.

As she walked, gazing at the flat horizon that seemed to go on forever, she thought about Sam helping with the harvest, laughing and joking with the guys who drove the combines and those who unloaded the grain. When would he have gotten a chance to do that in San Diego? When would Emily have had the chance to bond with a colt? Or Christopher the chance to chase barn cats?

She thought of their morning at church. Even though the kids weren't thrilled to be there, they sat through the service and listened to a man of God share about the gospel. The creek flowed beside her in near silence, and she pictured the boys this morning dressed in their good clothes, singing her favorite hymns. Their words were unsure, as they stumbled and tried to match their voices to the melody around them, but they'd been singing to God.

And Emily. She'd sat next to Bob, grandfather and granddaughter sharing a hymnal. The memory brought a soft smile to her lips. Her mind had been occupied with too many other things to take notice this morning. In fact, if it wasn't for this time of reflection, she would have missed the miracles happening around her.

"You're being awfully quiet. You okay?" Bob's voice wasn't much more than a whisper.

"Deep in thought, that's all. Thinking about your words and how right you are. Thinking about how the kids would do much better if we involved them, prepared them, instead of only doing for them." She sighed. "The barn it is."

Bob nodded. Charlotte thought back to the scene in the barn the other day, and laughter burst from her lips.

"What's so funny?" Bob released her hand and placed an arm around her shoulders.

"Oh, I was just thinking of the bats and of Emily's insistence that we remove them unharmed. Maybe after joining them for a sleepover, she won't complain so much about our methods of removal."

Bob's laughter joined hers. Then together, as if sensing that things *would* be all right, they turned toward home.

On the walk back, they chatted about everything and nothing in particular. When they neared the path through the pasture, Charlotte's eyes focused on their two-story, white clapboard house and the branches of the poplar trees surrounding it, swaying in the breeze.

Even though she couldn't see them, she heard the sounds of Toby's barking and Christopher's laughter. She pictured her grandson swinging on the tire swing Bob had made for Jennifer and Madison. With every swing, Toby would follow the tire and bark. Back and forth, back and forth. Toby never tired of the game, but Christopher usually found something new after a few minutes. For the moment, though, it was happy laughter and happy barking.

The farm smelled earthy and slightly sweet this time of year. Charlotte glanced up at her husband. He seemed even more at home here in the fields than in his recliner in the living room.

Sensing her gaze, Bob looked down at her. His hazel eyes spoke more than his words ever would. He was trying. He did care.

She knew all the changes at once were hard on him. She also knew he'd never stop loving her. Never stop loving his family.

"These are supposed to be the sunset years ... things slowing down, life getting easier, more quiet time." She wrinkled her nose.

"Well, think of it this way. We get to share our sunset with a whole passel of people."

Charlotte sighed. "How romantic."

"Actually, it sort of is. Those kids are a part of us, Charlotte. I can see bits of Denise in them." Bob's voice was thick and deep, hinting of his emotion. "In Christopher's observation of the world around him. In Emily's kindness with animals and her care for her friends."

"And what about Sam?"

Bob scratched his eyebrow.

Charlotte tapped her lip as a new thought struck her. "You know what? I just figured something out. Sam's like you."

"Like me?"

"He keeps things inside, mulling around in his head, and he's slow to let others in." She glanced at Bob and noticed his frown.

"Don't jump to conclusions. Let me finish." She bumped his arm with hers. "When he cares for something, he cares for it with everything in him, and—" She thought of Sam's pitiful report. She thought of Bob's combine.

"And?"

"He fights change," she said in barely a whisper.

"What's that?" Bob cupped his hand around this ear.

She looked up in the sky, noticing the gathering clouds on the western horizon. "It looks like rain." She lifted her hand, palm up. "Thirty minutes must be up. Don't you think it looks like rain, Bob?"

Chapter
Seventeen

Christopher pumped and pumped his legs, causing the swing to go higher into the sky. Toby ran back and forth next to him barking. Christopher imagined a bark like that most likely carried all the way to the clouds.

He heard the sound of a truck door slamming shut and jumped from the swing. Uncle Pete had driven his truck out to fix a fence. Whatever that meant.

Christopher had asked if he could go along, but Uncle Pete had said he had some thinking to do. Christopher didn't understand that at all. His uncle had to think to drive, to fix fence, and to check on the cows. It's not like anyone could *stop* thinking.

But now he was back. Maybe they could watch another *Star Wars* movie. He ran toward the truck. Toby tagged after him.

Uncle Pete was pulling some tools out of the back of his truck. He looked in Christopher's direction but didn't seem to see him. Christopher knew his mom used to have that look when she was thinking hard. Maybe when he got to be an adult thinking would be harder than it was now.

Christopher skipped down the sidewalk. Every time he did he made sure to miss the cracks, which was hard because there were a lot. Toby trotted by his side.

"Uncle Pete?" The sidewalk ended in gravel, and Christopher ran up to his uncle's side. Then he glanced up to the apartment windows over the garage. "Can I sleep over at your house tonight? I like you and Betty."

"I thought you were sleeping in the barn tonight."

"Yeah, I guess so." His stomach felt all jumpy and funny when he thought about sleeping in the barn. It was the same type of feeling he had when he had to go to Bedford Elementary that first day.

"You change your mind?"

"Well, what if something does come? The only fighting Sam knows how to do is on video games, and Emily is a girl. She'll probably run."

"You're probably right, but I've made a deal with Grandpa. I told him I'd stay up and listen for you. He thinks it's animals too—most likely coons. This isn't the first time we've had trouble with them in the garden."

Christopher followed his Uncle Pete to the barn, watching as his uncle put a loop of wire stuff on the wall and the cutter thing on a hook.

Christopher looked around the barn, reminding himself it didn't look *too* scary. In fact it looked kind of fun. He tried to imagine what it would be like to sleep there in the dark. Did the milk cows snore? Were there really bats in the rafters like Emily said?

He kicked his foot against a clump of straw on the ground and imagined sleeping on the stuff. He also imagined writing a letter to his old teacher Mrs. Falle—the one who used to read *Little House on the Prairie* to the class. He could write and tell her that he'd slept in a *real barn.*

Christopher imagined her reading his letter to the class just as she'd read Laura's story. The thought made him smile.

"Okay, I'll sleep in here." Christopher blurted out.

Uncle Pete turned from where he was straightening some tools on hooks. "I wasn't trying to talk you into it. If you're not comfortable—"

"No, I'm comfortable," Christopher interrupted.

"Okay, then, grublet. We can plan for you to sleep over at my place on another night. Maybe on a weekend, a non-school night. Then we can stay up late and watch *all* the *Star Wars* movies."

"Deal!" Christopher lifted a hand in the air, and Uncle Pete gave him a high five.

Grublet. Grublet. The word played over in Christopher's mind as he skipped toward the door of the barn.

"Uncle Pete?" He paused and turned. "What's a grublet?"

Uncle Pete laughed. "It's a little white worm that eats rotten garbage."

Christopher nodded and then raced out of the barn to pack. "Grublet. Cool."

Chapter
Eighteen

Despite her conversation with Bob, Charlotte was still uncertain about letting the kids sleep out in the barn on a school night. It was bad enough they most likely would stay up too late and would be irritable in the morning. Even worse, she wasn't convinced it was animals making a mess in the garden. The fact that Pete would keep an eye on things from his apartment didn't help either. As if he'd be able to stay up. Pete worked hard, played hard, and slept even harder.

When they arrived back from their walk, Bob headed off in the truck to check the fences Pete had fixed. Charlotte harvested more vegetables from the garden—putting them up before something else got ahold of them. She knelt on her foam board, picking the last of the beans. In the distance, she could see Emily and Sam near the horse corral. It looked like Emily had just finished brushing Stormy's coat and was putting everything away. Charlotte had to admit Emily had a natural way with horses, just like Denise at that age.

Not far from the garden, Pete was hacking away at one of the tree's unruly limbs. Near him, Christopher watched the small limbs fall and then he hurried to drag them into a burn pile near the back fence. He took his job seriously, making sure not a twig was left on the ground.

"How old are you, Uncle Pete?" Christopher gazed up in awe at his uncle.

Pete balanced on a ladder and stretched his arms forward, reaching for a far limb. "Your age times three, plus two."

Christopher balled his fists and scrunched his nose, feigning anger over the fact Pete was actually making him solve a math problem instead of just giving an answer.

Charlotte chuckled to herself and turned her attention back to the beans.

After a few seconds Christopher answered. "Thirty-two?"

"Yup. A-plus for you."

"Yeah, but if you're that old how come you don't have any kids? My mom was only three years older than that and she had three kids."

"Maybe because I haven't found a wife yet."

"Think about it." It was Emily's voice as she strode by. Charlotte guessed she was done putting away the horse's brush. "It's not like he can just go to the feed store and buy one. I'd like a wife and a bucket of chicken feed, please."

Emily's face displayed a smirk. She sat down cross-legged on the grass under the tree and made quick work of braiding her blonde hair without benefit of mirror or brush.

"Listen to you, *Californian*. Don't be so quick to judge the feed store. Did people around your Golden State go to the mall to pick up a husband or wife?" Pete leaned down, keeping one hand on a limb for balance. "Actually, maybe they did. Like the latest fashion statement. Take off the old wife, put on a new one."

"Pete, that's enough." Charlotte's voice was firm. Sometimes her son didn't think about what he was saying. He didn't remember these three kids came from a broken home. Bringing up their parents' divorce wouldn't help anything. Pete snipped at a branch and it tumbled to the ground.

Christopher ran for it, then paused. "I heard that you used to date Sam's teacher," he called to his uncle.

"Yeah, Miss Simons," Emily added.

Charlotte looked around for Sam, wondering where he'd gone. She didn't see him near the corral or barn. She didn't see him anywhere. *Maybe he just went inside to get a snack.* That boy seemed to have a hollow leg.

"That was a long time ago," Pete said quietly.

She could hear the sound of Christopher's running, dragging the branch behind him. A moment later, he returned. "Sam says she asked why you weren't married yet."

"Didn't either," Pete mumbled, yet Charlotte noted a note of interest in his voice.

"Did too," Emily jumped in. "I was there when she said it."

Charlotte glanced up in time to see that Emily had finished her braid and tied it off with a rubber band.

"Maybe you should marry her, Uncle Pete," Christopher said as nonchalantly as if he'd suggested they have hot dogs for dinner.

"Well, grublet, I'll think about that, but I'm not sure. Girls are complicated."

"Yeah, but then you can have cool kids. Just look at me and Sam and Emily. Mom used to say some of the hardest stuff ends up being some of the best."

"Ma, did you hear that?" Pete called. "We have a regular Confucius."

"Con, confoof who?" Christopher scratched his chin.

"A very wise man who lived long ago," Charlotte answered. She scooted her knee mat down to the next row of bean plants.

"Oh, was he one of the ones who went to visit baby Jesus, taking him a birthday gift?"

Pete laughed so hard Charlotte thought he was going to fall off the ladder. Charlotte's laughter joined his.

"What?" she heard Christopher ask. "What's so funny?"

DARKNESS HAD DESCENDED on the farm, dinner was done, the green beans were rinsed and bagged up, and the moment Charlotte dreaded had come. She heard Christopher's feet plodding down the stairway, and she glanced up from the calendar spread on the table before her. She'd been busy marking the half days, vacation days, and special events for the next few months. And wondering when she'd ever have time for herself above and beyond the kids' busy schedule.

Christopher stepped into the kitchen with his pillow and quilt in hand. Chewbacca hung from his arm and his Spider-Man backpack hung on his back, so stuffed it wasn't able to zip closed.

"Wow, you look like you're off for a long trip. You heading to Canada for vacation, or just to the barn?"

"Canada!" Christopher announced with a smile. Then he tapped his finger on his chin. "Grandma, where's Canada?"

"It's north of us. But since I don't have the time to draw you a good map, maybe you should just head to the barn for the night."

"Okay." Christopher went outside, and Toby—who'd been snoozing outside the back door—joined him. Charlotte considered following Christopher out. She could help him create a place for his sleeping bag from clean straw and take a look around the yard just in case. But then she remembered Bob's words. The kids needed to take ownership of this farm. They needed to feel a part of it. They were here for the long haul, and her tagging around and butting in wasn't going to help anything.

A few minutes later, Emily bounded down the stairs. A pair of binoculars hung around her neck. She had a sleeping bag tucked under one arm and a flashlight in each hand.

Charlotte placed her hands on her hips. "Well, hello there, Nancy Drew."

Emily smiled at the reference. "Whatever is out there, we're going to find it! Uncle Pete says he'll even stay up and keep watch from his window in case we fall asleep."

"Did you set some traps?"

"Yup, I made them myself. I used some old twine and old cans that Grandpa gave me. I strung them up all over the barn and if anything runs into them we'll hear the cans clanging together."

"Sounds like a plan to me."

Emily moved to the door.

"Emily, wait." Charlotte rose and hurried to the fridge. "I packed some snacks for tonight."

Emily took the paper sack from Charlotte's hands. Her eyes widened. "Sweet! Thanks, Grandma!" She leaned forward and offered Charlotte a peck on the cheek, then hurried out the door.

Charlotte placed her hand on the spot and smiled.

Chapter
Nineteen

Christopher curled up inside his sleeping bag. Though the air was cold, he was warm in his pajamas with Sam and Emily on either side of him. Grandma told him to get some sleep because he had school tomorrow, but he was too excited to try, and he had too much energy from the Rice Krispy treats his grandma had packed in the snack bag. He could tell from his brother's breathing that Sam was awake too, even though his eyes were closed.

Christopher commented every now and then about the noises in the barn, the sounds of the animals at night, the creak of the wind in the trees, but neither Sam nor Emily answered.

He remembered the first time he'd walked into the barn. It was big, bigger than he'd expected. And up above, it had a high hayloft—one that you'd need a parachute to jump down from. It also had a big open space. Emily had told Christopher that in olden days they'd held square dances in places just like this.

Now the darkness made the place seem like a big black hole, just like the ones in outer space. He hugged Chewbacca closer.

"Can I have a turn?" Christopher reached a hand into the cold air toward the binoculars Emily had been pressing to her face for hours. He giggled to himself, imagining Emily with raccoon eyes in the morning from looking through those things.

"In a minute. I think I see something."

Christopher sighed. "That's what you said ten minutes ago."

"Shhhh. In a minute."

She pointed the binoculars to the garden.

Toby snuggled close, and Christopher noticed cockleburs in the fur around her paws. He took one front paw and placed it on his pillow. Then he tugged on the cockleburs, pulling them free. A few of those little stickers were stuck real good, and he had to yank hard. Toby didn't seem to mind. She barely opened her eyes and watched with curiosity.

When he finished, Emily still had those binoculars pressed to her face.

"You should look up. Maybe you'll see somethin' up there." *Maybe somethin' coming down from outer space.* He wondered if the spaceships in real life looked like the ones in *Star Wars.*

He rolled onto his back and stared through the open crack of the barn door at the dark sky and the Christmas-light stars that blinked at him. When Emily didn't comment, Christopher poked her arm.

"I said look up. I think that's where they're coming from."

"Um-hum," Emily said. It was the same thing she said every time she pretended to listen but really didn't.

It didn't matter though. She would know he was right soon enough.

"Sam." Christopher turned to his side. "Is the sky closer to Nebraska than it is in San Diego?"

"Nope. Same difference." Sam wore a dirty ball cap. It reminded him of one Uncle Pete wore, but Uncle Pete's cap was blue and Sam's was red. Yet instead of wearing it above his eyebrows like Uncle Pete did, Sam had it lowered over his eyes as he pretended to sleep.

"But this sky looks different. The stars look closer. It looks bigger too."

"That's 'cause in San Diego all the lights from the city make it hard to see the stars."

From beside Christopher, Toby stirred. She lifted her head. Before they came to live on the farm, Grandma said Toby had always slept outside, but on most nights she now slept inside his room. Lightning preferred to sleep on Grandpa's recliner, but Christopher usually waited until he heard Grandma and Grandpa stop talking—their muffled voices no longer coming through the heating vent—and he'd let Toby into his room.

He was glad no one asked why the dog hadn't barked the two days when someone or something had come to take things. Then he'd have to admit it was because Toby was with him instead of protecting the farm. Of course, even if she'd been outside Christopher wasn't sure Toby would hear whoever had gotten in the garden. Maybe aliens were super-silent.

But now Toby heard something for sure. Her ears perked up and a low growl sounded in her throat.

"What is it, girl?" Sam sat up, pushing his blanket off him.

Toby jumped up onto her feet. Before Sam could grab her collar, the dog bolted from the door, heading toward the garden. She barked wildly, and Christopher heard Emily's cans banging together.

"I told you I saw something!" Emily jumped to her feet, but she didn't rush forward. She stood there and looked at Sam and Christopher as if wondering what to do.

Sam jumped up too. Without a word, he grabbed a shovel from the wall and ran out, following Toby. Ten seconds later, a man's cry split the air.

Emily stared at Christopher. "Who is that?" Her eyes were as big as the binocular lenses she held in her hand.

"Should we go see what it is?" he asked.

She grabbed two flashlights from under her pillow, turned one on and handed it to Christopher. Then she turned on the second one for herself.

Christopher swallowed hard. A second shout split the air. It was Pete's voice. He was saying something, but it was too low and too far away for Christopher to understand.

Christopher tugged on Emily's arm. "Uncle Pete must have heard them too! Maybe he saw them from his window. Come on. It sounds like Uncle Pete and Sam caught 'em!"

The two hurried out. The flashlight beams bounced on the ground in front of them—two thin streams of light in the middle of all the darkness, and for the first time Christopher wondered if it was a good idea to meet a space alien face-to-face.

He swallowed hard, grabbed Emily's hand, and continued forward.

Up ahead they saw the garden and someone wriggling in the grass on the side of it. Voices carried to them through the night air.

"What did you have to do that for?" Pete was shouting at Sam.

"What do you mean? I thought you were a burglar. I was just protecting my brother and sister! What were you doing out here anyway?"

"Checking on *you*," Pete shouted. "I just wanted to make sure you guys were okay. I didn't know the yard was booby-trapped!"

They hurried forward, and Christopher shined his light on the thing on the grass. The light flashed in Pete's face, and he moaned again.

"Hey, kid, turn that thing off. You trying to blind me?"

Something was wrapped around Pete's legs and he was trying to unwrap them.

"Where are they?" Christopher excitedly asked, looking around.

"Who?"

Christopher didn't answer. Instead, he looked closer at Pete. He shined his flashlight on Pete's shoulder and noticed blood. "Uncle Pete, you're hurt!"

"Yeah, that's because someone caught me in a trap, and someone else tried to knock my head off! Good thing Sam's a bad aim . . ."

Toby licked at Pete's hand, and Pete pushed her away.

Pete mumbled something under his breath and tugged harder at the string. "Well, are you just going to stand there? Emily, run and get some scissors or something, so I can cut this twine. And Christopher, can you ask Grandma to get the first aid kit? I'm gonna need her to look at my shoulder."

Christopher and Emily hurried to the house. She stopped him at two different places, showing where she'd tied the twine and the cans. Christopher crawled under those spots with Emily right behind him. The grass was cold and wet, and by the time he got to the house he was shivering hard.

His hands trembled as he pounded on his grandparents' door. "Grandma, Grandma, come quick! Emily caught something in her trap!"

He could hear the noises inside the door of someone getting up. From behind him, he heard Emily in the kitchen looking through the junk drawer for scissors.

The door opened and the bedroom light flipped on. His grandma was standing at the door and Grandpa was sitting on the side of the bed in his pajamas. His hair was all messy and he had a confused look on his face.

"Emily caught Uncle Pete in her trap, and Sam didn't know it was him and hit him with the shovel!"

His grandma's eyes widened and her nostrils flared. "Fine, we'll be right out."

She closed the door with a slam, and Christopher turned to go help Emily find the scissors. And even though he walked away from the door, he could hear Grandma talking to Grandpa, saying something about a hare-brained idea.

Christopher's stomach felt sick, like he was going to throw up. For some reason he felt it was his fault. He thought about Grandma, and he realized that he'd never seen her get that mad before. His mom used to get mad when Emily took clothes from her closet, or when Sam stayed out too late, or when he didn't clean his room like she asked, but it was weird for Grandma to be mad.

He thought about the stories Sam used to tell about their dad. How both Mom and Dad used to fight all the time until one day he just didn't come home.

Christopher's stomach hurt even more at the thought of Grandpa leaving and not coming back. More than anything he wanted to run upstairs, crawl under his covers, and pretend this whole night hadn't happened.

Chapter
Twenty

Charlotte waved good-bye as Sam and Emily climbed out of the car and hurried toward the high school. She glanced at her watch, wondering if she had time to stop by Mel's Place for a cup of coffee. More than the caffeine, she needed to see a friendly face. Ashley's mom, Melody, always seemed to have a smile, no matter what. Charlotte wished she could be more like her.

But it was already after eight, and she expected Christopher would be up by now, wondering where everyone had gone.

She was just about to pull her car out of the parking space when she noticed Dana Simons crossing the street right in front of her. Charlotte offered a wave.

Dana smiled with recognition and turned in Charlotte's direction, hurrying toward her car. Charlotte rolled down the window.

Dana glanced at her watch and leaned down. "Charlotte, I was going to call you today . . . but this works even better." Her dark hair fell into her face, and she tucked it behind her ear. "I only have a minute—otherwise the *teacher's* going to be tardy today. But I want to talk to you even for a second. It's about Sam's grades."

140

"I had a feeling you were going to say that." Charlotte's hands tightened around the steering wheel. "And from the look in your eyes I assume it's not good news."

Dana rested her hand on the car door, pressing a stack of files to her chest. "I wish it was good news, I really do. But Sam has failed his second English quiz in a week." Dana shook her head. "I don't understand it. From talking to him, and even from the answers Sam gives in class, I know he's a smart kid," Dana said. "For some reason, he's not trying."

Charlotte sighed. "I know. I see the same thing. I just wish I knew what to do about it. I've scolded him. I've tried to encourage him. I've given him a second chance on more than one occasion, but I don't know what good it's going to do."

The ringing of the school bell carried to the street, and Dana patted Charlotte's arm. "I'm so sorry. I wish I had more time to talk. I just thought you'd want to know."

"Yes, thank you, I appreciate your taking the time."

And with a small wave she watched Dana hurry away.

The knot in Charlotte's stomach tightened, and she decided to skip the coffee and just head home. Besides, she doubted even coffee and a smiling face could pick her up. And as she drove, Dana's words mixed with the overwhelming emotions of the night's events: Emily's tears, Sam's sullen attitude, Christopher throwing up all over the kitchen, the gash in Pete's arm from the dirty shovel and his refusal to go to the emergency room. And Bob's silence as they all headed back to their own rooms for the few remaining hours of the night.

Mostly, Charlotte was discouraged by her own reaction,

her anger at Bob, when she *knew* that he was only trying to do best by the kids.

She'd tried to apologize this morning, but Bob hadn't responded. He'd only nodded and then headed out into the yard to clean up the mess that Emily had made with the twine and cans.

When she pulled into the driveway, the mess was cleaned up. Charlotte also noticed Christopher, on the porch, playing fetch with Toby. He was still in his pajamas and his feet were bare. He dropped the ball and ran back into the house when he saw her.

She found him inside a minute later, sitting on the couch and looking at one of his library books.

"Hey, champ. You feeling better?"

He glanced up and shrugged. "Guess so. How come you didn't get me up for school?"

She sat in Bob's chair, facing Christopher. "Well, you were pretty sick last night. Could have been from the extra snacks or all the excitement, but I thought it was better to be safe than sorry."

"I'm missing our group project. We were gonna work on our rock collection."

"I'm sure your teacher will understand. I'll write a note tomorrow."

His finger poked at a wear spot on the arm of the couch, and she opened her mouth to tell him not to make a bigger hole, but then changed her mind. There was a shadowed sadness in Christopher's look that told her something bothered him—something deep and more meaningful than a rock collection.

She rose and straightened the newspapers on the coffee table and adjusted the throw pillows on the couch. She also noticed that Christopher's eyes were on her every move.

"Where's Grandpa?" he finally said, gazing out the window, looking beyond the yard to the pasture.

"I'm not sure, but he's around here somewhere. Maybe we can take a walk and find him." She approached and touched his forehead. It felt neither too hot nor too cold. "After all, it looks like you're feeling better."

"What if we can't?" He hugged his legs to his chest.

"Can't what?"

"Find him."

Charlotte felt her brow furrow. "You mean . . ."

Christopher's lower lip trembled and for the first time she noticed dark circles under his eyes.

"Christopher? Did you hear Grandpa and me arguing last night after the accident with Pete?"

"Yeah. I guess so."

"Are you worried that because Grandpa and I argued, that he's going to leave?"

Christopher didn't say anything. She sat down on the couch beside him.

"Oh, honey, that's not going to happen. Everyone argues and fights now and then, but that doesn't mean Grandpa's going to leave. He's made a commitment to God and to me to stick around. Besides, he's also made a commitment to you, Sam, and Emily. He wants you here. I want you here."

"So, he really *is* just out in the field, or something?"

"Yes, he is. He's most likely checking the cows, making

sure they're all healthy. Or maybe he even walked down to Heather Creek. That's where Grandpa goes sometimes to talk to God."

"Is God at the creek?"

"Yes, and He's at the barn, and in the yard, in San Diego, and even the North Pole. God is everywhere, but there are some places we feel Him best. In fact, God is right here, with us, right now. What do you think about us praying and asking God to make you feel better, and to help me not to act like I did last night? Does that sound good to you?"

Christopher nodded and scooted closer so his head rested on her shoulder.

"Dear God," she began, her heart feeling both humble and full, "sometimes we need You so much. And, Lord, this is one of those times."

Chapter Twenty-One

Christopher yawned as he hung his arm over his bed and dropped the book into a pile with the others he'd read.

He had spent some of the day helping Grandma clean the house. He liked using the feather duster, and Grandma gave him two dollars for helping. After that, he helped Uncle Pete outside. He even took a ride into town with Grandpa. But after he'd yawned a ton, Grandma told him he needed to rest for a while.

He had lain in his bed for what seemed like ten hours, and when he got bored he started reading. It was almost dark, and he wondered when Emily and Sam would come home, but still he didn't get up. The bed was warm and cozy, and the books were cool.

He'd looked through all the photos of airplanes, spacecraft, and motorcycle parts, and he had yet to find anything like his part. The light outside the window had dimmed to a warm glow, so he flipped on the lamp next to his bed and tilted the lampshade so it made a bright circle on his lap. He had one more book to go through before he headed back outside to help Uncle Pete with the night chores.

It was a book about old automobiles, but the lady at the library showed him it had lots of photos and drawings. He flipped through it and yawned again. But then, when it got to photos of vintage old car engines he slowed. There on the second page was a photo of a part just like his!

"Car-bur-e-tor." He sounded out the word, and he thought he'd heard of it before. It might have been the thing that broke on their old car—the one his mom used to drive. It made him sad to think of his mom in that old blue clunker, and he made those thoughts go away just like he wiped the fog from the bathroom mirror after a shower.

"Carburetor," he said again. He pressed the open book to his chest and raced down the stairs.

His feet flew so fast he wasn't sure he hit every step. In a blur, he saw his grandma in the kitchen, mixing something in her big old blender. The air smelled of cinnamon and some other sweet stuff, but he didn't pause.

"Going out to help Uncle Pete!" he called as he slipped on his shoes and pushed on the screen door, hearing the faintest thud as it slammed shut behind him.

He glanced around, noticing the yard was empty, and scurried over to the shed. He set the book outside the door on the dirt and scrambled inside, moving the bucket. He found his treasure. He pulled it out and then set it on the ground next to the book. He'd been almost sure before, but seeing the two side by side he knew now this was what he'd found. But what was it doing in that field?

A bark broke the air, and Christopher noticed Toby racing toward him, head lowered and legs stretched like she did most times Christopher ventured out. Before Christopher could stop her, Toby jumped up on him, happily giving him a wet lick on his cheek. Toby's front feet pawed Christopher's chest and her back ones jumped on the book, leaving smears of mud. He tried to push the dog back.

"Toby, watch out, girl, you're gonna—"

Rip. The sound of the book's page tearing caused Christopher to push harder against the dog. "Toby, no, now look what you've done!"

He picked up the book and tried to brush it off. *Rip.* The page tore even more. "Toby . . ." He moved to the back door and set the book on a crate someone had stacked there. Making a note to himself to clean it up and tape it later, he ran back and picked up the metal *carburetor* and hurried to the barn.

Uncle Pete sat on a stool in front of one of the milk cows. His Nebraska Cornhuskers cap was pulled low, causing two flaps of his hair to flip out over his ears, making them look like mini angel wings. Of course Christopher would never tell Uncle Pete that—he wasn't the angel type of person.

"Uncle Pete, look." Christopher raced up to where his uncle sat. The cow let out a low moo as if bothered by the disruption.

"It's okay, Trudy." He patted the cow's black-and-white side, which was more black than white.

Christopher stretched out his hands, holding the carburetor out as if he was holding a crown for a king. "Look what I found." Christopher grinned.

Pete turned his attention to Christopher. One eyebrow shot up. "What you got there, squirt?"

"I found this in the field. It's part of an old car. Do you know how it got in the field?"

"Not a clue, but don't you go leaving that piece of junk

around the barn. I just cleaned this place up and now my shoulder *really* hurts."

"Piece of junk?" Christopher felt his shoulders slump. "It's not a piece of junk. It's like all those old things Grandma collects, an—an . . ."

"Antique? That's not an antique. See how rusty it is?"

"But, Uncle Pete . . ." Christopher's voice rose, and Trudy mooed again, lifting a back foot as if trying to push Uncle Pete away.

"Listen. It is junk, and you're upsetting Trudy. Now why don't you throw it in the back of the truck, and I'll take it in the next run to the dump. Okay?"

Christopher slowly nodded but he had no intention of throwing it away. It was a piece of history, something from the past. More than that, it was a mystery to be solved. He *would* find out what a car part was doing in the middle of the meadow.

"So, I thought you were going to help me with the chores tonight? I could really use a hand."

"Yeah, I was gonna." Christopher pushed out his chest. "I'll go put this away, and then I'll help."

Christopher hurried back outside, hoping he wasn't lying. He was going to put it away—just not where Uncle Pete thought. Glancing around to make sure no one else was in the yard or the barn area, Christopher hurried back into the shed and slid the carburetor behind the bucket.

He'd figure it out. He already knew what it was and what kind of machine it came from. Half of the mystery was already solved.

He'd show them. He'd show them all.

Chapter Twenty-Two

Charlotte pressed the edges of the crust with her moist finger, adding a crinkled ring around the edge of the pie plate. Then she slid it into the oven, checking to make sure she'd set the right temperature.

She glanced out the window and wondered when Bob would come in. He was out checking the corn and making a plan for harvest. She knew that as soon as he entered the kitchen he'd be able to tell something else was gnawing at her gut, like dozens of field mice chewing a hole in a grain sack.

What can I do about Sam's schoolwork, Lord? Charlotte had prayed through the apple cinnamon bread and the berry pie, but she still didn't have an answer. She hoped Bob would come home in time for them to talk it through before the kids got back, but he hadn't.

Not that she couldn't guess what he'd say: "We'll pile on more chores and show him what hard work is all about." Of course hard work was good, but that method hadn't worked with Pete.

She'd even called Bill to get his advice. He'd always worked hard at his schoolwork and applied himself. She thought maybe he'd have an answer, but when she called Bill's cell phone he answered just long enough to tell her he was in a meeting and he'd call her later. So here she was with a week's worth of cleaning and baking done, but still no answers.

Melody's car, carrying the older kids, stopped outside, and she watched as Emily and Sam climbed out. They'd stayed in town late to help decorate the high school for Spirit Week, and Melody had promised to give them a ride home. Charlotte waved out the window, but she wasn't sure if Melody saw her. Then Charlotte watched as the teens made their way to the back porch.

Emily was talking a mile a minute, seeming not to care that Sam wasn't answering. Beside her, Sam walked hunched over with his hands in his pockets, his backpack slipped over his shoulder, and his sweatshirt hood pulled over his head.

They entered the door and Emily hurried to the counter. "Ohh . . . can I have a cookie, Grandma?"

"Just one, and then I need you to finish cleaning your room. Your bed wasn't made, and your dirty clothes, amazingly, must have jumped out of the hamper and scattered themselves all over the floor."

"But I'll be getting back in bed in a few hours." Emily pouted.

"That's not the point. The point is that you're supposed to do it before you leave in the morning and you didn't."

"Phooey." Emily let out a quick breath and blew her bangs from her face. "Fine," she said, taking a cookie and hustling up the stairs.

Sam hung his backpack on a hook by the back door and looked as if he was going to escape outside without saying a word when Charlotte wagged a finger his direction. "Not so fast, young man. I think there's some stuff we need to talk about."

Sam turned and pushed his hands deep in the pockets of his ratty jeans. "What stuff?"

"How 'bout failing two quizzes?"

"Hey, you can't blame me. History's nothing but dumb ol' names and dates."

"I was talking about English. But thanks for letting me know about history too."

Sam pulled his hands from his pockets and shrugged. "Man, this town is lame. I can't even cross my eyes without someone calling my grammy. In San Diego the teachers didn't even know my name."

"Yes, well, this isn't San Diego. And they call because they care. You're smart and your teachers don't want to see you fail. You can do better, if you'll just apply yourself."

"Yeah, whatever. Whatever you say . . ." Instead of going outside, he hurried up the stairs, his long legs stretching, skipping every other one.

Charlotte threw her hands up in the air. She moved to the dining room and slumped into the chair just as the phone rang.

"Hello," she answered less than enthusiastically.

"Hey, I have dinner in the Crock-Pot, and I was wondering if you'd want to take a quick walk before the men come in for supper." Charlotte recognized the voice of her dear friend and neighbor Hannah Carter. "I know your evenings have been full and all, with helping the kids with their schoolwork. I thought I'd try to catch you when I could."

Charlotte thought about the rock collection she still had to help Christopher organize and the library books she had to gather up before she headed into town tomorrow. She also thought about the hamburger she was going to brown for tacos. She'd gotten the rest of the fixings ready, but hadn't had time to do that . . . Yet, there was always something. Her list never ended. But, Charlotte sighed, she could sure use a listening ear.

"So what do you think?" Hannah asked, prodding for an answer.

"Sure, head on over. I can go for a quick walk. And if dinner's ten minutes late I think my family will live."

My family. Yes, Charlotte heard herself use that word to describe Bob, Pete, *and* the kids. She knew this situation was for the long haul, which is why she needed to get this problem with Sam figured out. She'd given him time and space, and now she needed answers.

Hannah showed up less than ten minutes later with a paper plate of chocolate chip cookies covered by Saran Wrap. Laughter burst from her lips as she eyed the kitchen counter filled with various other baked goods.

"Honey, it looks like you don't need those cookies, but I'll leave them all the same. They're Christopher's favorite recipe." She placed them on the counter and pressed her fists into her hips. "But it does look like you need to talk." She offered Charlotte a quick hug.

"Remember," she whispered in Charlotte's ear. "Whatever it is, we'll make it through this too, just like times past." Charlotte nodded and tied up her walking shoes. When Toby saw the two were headed out the door, the faithful dog joined them.

Charlotte was silent until they reached the gravel road and then the words spilled along with a few wayward tears. "I just don't know what to do about Sam. He's failing English, and it sounds like history too," she said, shaking her head. "I've tried to encourage him to study. I've thought about grounding him, but what do I take away, chores? I've asked Bob to talk to him, but stubborn plus stubborn doesn't make for peace, or a solution. I'm at my wit's end, and I'm afraid that Sam's going to follow in Pete's footsteps and drop out because trying is just too much effort."

Hannah's arms swung at her sides and her feet matched Charlotte's pace. She was quiet and Charlotte knew she was thinking it through, letting the responses spin through her head like a hamster on a wheel, and Charlotte was glad for that. It seemed everyone in town wanted to give Charlotte advice about raising kids in this generation. She appreciated the fact that Hannah actually thought her advice through before she spoke.

"Okay, it does sound like you've tried everything, and you should be commended for that." The wind blew straight on, and Hannah brushed a gray strand back from her face. "But I think there is one thing you haven't tried, and that is to let Sam fail."

Charlotte stopped short. Overhead a flock of geese flew

by, heading south. Their honking echoed over the expansive land around them.

"Let him fail?"

"Sure. In the end he's the one who will have to face the consequences. Like the time the crew from *Gilligan's Island* decided to go for a second cruise after being rescued. They didn't learn the first time, and they just found themselves in the same place. Sam's decisions will lead to Sam's consequences. He knows that. But he also figures that you'll keep doing what you've been doing—helping him by making it okay and by making allowances. But if you give him the freedom to fail, then he has to face up to the bad choices he's making."

"You mean I shouldn't talk to Sam when Miss Simons calls? I shouldn't make a plan? I shouldn't remind him about his homework?"

"That's exactly what I'm saying."

"That's easier said than done."

Hannah continued on, and Charlotte hurried to catch up.

"I never said it would be easy."

"Hmm . . ." Charlotte said, letting the advice play over in her mind. "Yeah, well, I'll think about it."

She thought a few more minutes as the gravel road rose slightly. Charlotte thought about it as Hannah talked about the quilt project she was starting for next year's county fair. She only half listened. She thought about it as they turned back, and as she saw the farm from a distance. From this far away, it looked so peaceful, so quaint and perfect.

In the end, while Charlotte appreciated Hannah's advice, she didn't think she could follow through with it. She couldn't let Sam fail. What would his teachers say? How would she be honoring Denise's memory? She couldn't leave Sam up to his own devices, especially if they led to no good. This time around, things were different. She had to make things work. She'd seen what happened to those who didn't apply themselves, and to those who did. *Sam cannot fail*, she told herself as Hannah veered off toward her farm with a wave. *Sam cannot fail.*

Charlotte continued on back to her farm.

This time there has to be another way.

This time I have to do better.

This time I have to make things work.

The future of her grandson—her grandchildren, all of them—counted on it.

⌣ Chapter Twenty-Three

Charlotte sprinkled taco seasoning on the hamburger frying in the skillet. She also stirred the refried beans on the stove and opened the oven to check on the tortillas that were warming. Bean burritos for Emily and tacos for the rest of the crew. Her stomach growled, and she realized that besides a few nibbles of baked goods here and there, she hadn't eaten much today.

Christopher and Emily sat in the living room, watching *Wheel of Fortune* with Bob and trying to guess the correct responses. Sam sat at the dining room table with something that appeared, amazingly, like homework. Pete was outside, visiting with some of the guys from the combine crew. It seemed like he enjoyed their company—guys his age to talk farming with.

The microwave beeped, telling Charlotte that the cold cup of coffee she was reheating was done.

"Grandma, who's Fred Astaire?"

"What did you just ask?" She glanced at Sam as she grabbed the mug from the microwave. The hot liquid splashed over the edge, burning her thumb.

"Ouch," she mumbled, placing the mug on the counter.

"You know, Fred Astaire? That famous guy. Who is he?"

"Well, he was a singer, dancer, and actor. I remember him from some of the movies when I was a kid."

"Just wondering."

"Just wondering? Next, you're gonna be asking about Ginger Rogers . . ."

"Who? Oh, wait, is she the one from those old *Gilligan's Island* reruns?"

Charlotte chuckled. "No, she was a dancer too. She danced with Fred Astaire."

"Gin-ger Rog-ers." Sam wrote the name on the paper in front of him.

Charlotte wiped her hands on her apron and strolled over to the counter. "What *are* you doing?"

"Working on the report. The Nebraska, aren't-we-the-best-state-ever report. I don't know why, though. I'm still going to fail."

Thank You, Lord! Charlotte's heart did a double beat.

"Why do you say that you're going to fail? Let me see what you have."

"So far just a lot of boring dates and stuff."

Charlotte's eyes scanned down the page.

NEBRASKA

In Nebraska, most of the land is used by farmers. Top crops are corn, wheat, and soybeans. It's called the Cornhusker State. A cornhusker is someone who harvests or "husks" corn by hand.

Nebraska is the fifteenth largest state. Severe weather can include flooding in the spring, tornadoes in the summer, and blizzards in the winter. The state capital is Lincoln, and the average July temperature is seventy-six degrees. The average January temperature is twenty-three, and I'm sure I've never been in a place that cold in my life.

Charlotte chuckled at the last statement and kept reading.

Omaha is the largest city, and it was once considered the gateway to the west. Pioneers crossed Nebraska going west in the 1880s. Chimney Rock was a famous landmark on the Oregon Trail.

In 1862, President Abraham Lincoln signed the Homestead Act. The act said people could have 160 acres of public land for free. It was available to any person who was the head of a household and at least twenty-one years old. Thousands of settlers came to Nebraska.

Famous Nebraskans are Gerald Ford, a former president, and Fred Astaire, a dancer. Fred Astaire danced with Ginger Rogers. The next famous Nebraskan will be soccer star Sam Slater, who will be even greater than David Beckham.

Charlotte smiled at that. "David Beckham, huh?"
Sam nodded. "Keep going."

The weather changes a lot in Nebraska. It is warm and sunny one minute and cold and hailing the next. Nebraska was part of the Louisiana Purchase.

"Well, it seems like you do have a lot of the facts." Charlotte glanced into Sam's hopeful face. "And your spelling is great."

"Anything I need to fix?" he asked.

"Well, I do think that some of the parts can be reorganized. For example, you can put all the parts about the weather in the same paragraph . . . and maybe all the history stuff together too." She pointed to the paper. "See, this part about the Louisiana Purchase might go better up here."

Sam nodded and scribbled on his paper, making an arrow to the top.

"And . . ." She searched Sam's face to see if she dared to give more advice. He looked at her expectantly, and he truly seemed to be interested in her comments.

"And, all the stats you gave, well, you could do that with any state," she added. "I think what could really help you is to talk to some more people and get their ideas. Maybe why they love it here? What they remember if they grew up in these parts? For example, when I was little there were still people around who had soddies on their property."

"Soddies?" Sam's hair hung nearly to his eyes. It shagged over his ears, making him look more like an innocent puppy than a rebellious teen. Warmth filled her chest and she felt like brushing the hair back from his face. It was a sweet moment, seeing the tenderness in his gaze. She'd seen it only a few times before, like when he spoke with Christopher and sometimes with Emily.

Charlotte knew she needed to finish browning the hamburger, but she didn't want to break the moment. She ignored the ticking clock and glanced down at the page.

"Yes, during that Homestead Act—" She pointed to the spot on his paper that talked about it. "Many settlers moved here with little to nothing. Most didn't have money to buy lumber for homes so they made little homes out of hard-packed sod. I remember riding with my dad on the gravel roads and thinking they looked like grassy warts sticking up in the fields. Over the years they crumbled and became little more than miniature hills, but I think it's part of our history that's worth repeating. Maybe . . ."

The screen door creaked open, and Pete entered. Sam glanced at his uncle and quickly slammed the book shut. He gave Pete the same wide-eyed look that a toddler gets when he's caught with his hand in the cookie jar.

"As I was saying . . ." Charlotte patted Sam's shoulder, as if urging him to stay seated. "There are lots of stories, lots of people from town you can talk to. They can give you some of the history—"

Sam brushed off her hand and rose. "Really, Grandma, I just want to get this done. It's not like I want to spend time talking to old pe—" He shrugged. "I mean, I don't think I need to go that far."

Emily sauntered into the kitchen. "Grandma, I think there is something we need to talk about."

"Well, I was helping Sam right now—"

Sam looked at Emily. "No, Emily, go ahead, we're done." He shoved his notebook into his backpack and tossed the backpack to the floor. Then Sam strolled into the living room, plopping onto the couch next to Christopher.

"Mashed potatoes and gravy!" Sam shouted at the screen, solving the puzzle at nearly the same time as the game show contestant. "Look, I just won ten grand!"

Charlotte moved back to the hamburger and stirred it. It

looked almost done. She handed Emily a hot pad and pointed to the table. "So what's up?" Charlotte glanced at Emily nonchalantly, but inside she felt as if worker bees were doing a dance within her chest. This was the first time Emily had come to Charlotte with her concerns, and it felt like a big step.

Emily placed it on the table. Then she turned and sighed. "It's Christopher. He has a strange fascination with all those books. I asked him what he was doing, and he told me he was looking for something, for parts. Do you think he wants to try to build something?"

"What can a ten-year-old build?" Charlotte asked.

"It's not what he *can* build. It's what he wants to build. All the books he's reading are on stuff from the past."

"What do you think he wants to build?"

Emily stared at the ceiling and shrugged. "Maybe a time machine?"

"What do you mean?" Charlotte turned down the burner and gave Emily her full attention.

"You know, something to take him back."

"Back?"

"To before. Before the stupid accident."

"How long have you been feeling like this?"

"It's not me, it's Christopher."

Charlotte motioned to the table. Emily sat in one of the chairs, and Charlotte sat across from her.

"Okay, why do you think *Christopher* wants to go back in time?"

Emily took the napkin from the side of the plate that

had been set up for dinner, and she began folding it until it was so small and thick it couldn't be folded any more.

"Maybe because he felt like he belonged in California, and he doesn't belong here. Remember how horrible that first day of school was for him? And what happened the other night...he was so scared that it made him sick. Maybe it just doesn't seem like he should be here, that's all."

"Wow, I never thought Christopher worried about all that. Can you tell him for me that you, he, and Sam have always been a part of our lives? Can you tell him your grandpa and I have prayed for the three of you every day? You've never been a stranger to me."

"Yeah, well, you could have fooled us. Sometimes I...we...forgot we even had grandparents." It wasn't hard to miss the snip in Emily's voice.

"I know we could have done things differently..."

Emily rose, pushing her hands out in front of her as if trying to block Charlotte's words.

"Listen, I don't need a sappy sympathy card, okay? Things are the way they are. I just thought you'd want to know about Christopher, that's all. I saw him running around today with an old piece of junk, and I thought it could be dangerous."

"Yeah, okay, thanks for letting me know."

Charlotte rose and returned to her hamburger. She scooped it from the frying pan into a metal bowl. With each scoop, she found comfort in the steady clinking of the bowl against the counter.

Emily still sat at the table. She didn't move but Charlotte heard her snuffle in a breath.

"A time machine, honestly," Charlotte mumbled as she placed all the food on the table. "Don't they think I'd be the first to climb in?"

She called everyone to dinner, and then they held hands to pray. Bob said the familiar words, but her mind was on the idea of going back to the past.

Yes, she missed Denise and wished her daughter were still alive but . . .

Charlotte looked at the faces around her. *But I'd really miss these kids.* A lump rose in her throat. They tested her, stretched her, but she couldn't imagine life without them. What had she done before they arrived to occupy her time? Sure, she'd embroidered and cooked and helped with the animals, but those things paled when compared to seeing the kids growing and changing, inside and out.

"Charlotte? Would you like some beans?" Bob asked, passing her the bowl.

"You know what?" She smiled. "I'd love some . . . and I think I'm even going to try Emily's vegetarian version for a change."

Chapter
Twenty-Four

By the time the kids awoke the next morning and got ready for school the thunderheads had rumbled in. Charlotte eyed the sky and noticed how they cast long gray shadows across the house and yard and meadow beyond. She buttoned her sweater, noting a chill in the air, then shut the kitchen window, opened just a crack. It felt like Indian summer was finally coming to an end.

Toby trotted down the stairs from Christopher's room and whined at the door to go out. Charlotte wordlessly let her out, smiling at the thought that Christopher still believed she didn't know he sneaked the dog into his room most nights. The cool air smelled of rain, and the clouds rumbled overhead as if the sky was clearing its throat. Outside, she could faintly make out Pete in the barn pitching fresh hay into the stalls. Bob sauntered up and shouted something to his son. Charlotte couldn't make out the words as they were lost in a gust of wind. Rain meant mud, and mud meant more laundry.

Charlotte sighed as she headed to the washer and the pile of clothes in front of it. She sorted them, separating the darks, the towels, and the whites, wondering how kids who claimed they had nothing to wear had so many dirty clothes.

She tossed Emily's jeans skirt in with Sam's frayed and holey cargo pants. She lifted up Christopher's jeans, diligently checking the pockets. Today's quest yielded a half-eaten apple, which he'd most likely shared with one of the milk cows, an old key, a link from a chain, and a funny-shaped rock. She tossed the apple into the trash and plunked the rest of the items into an old coffee can she used to save Christopher's treasures. Already in the can was a linchpin, nuts, a bolt, an acorn, and a rusty screwdriver.

"Grandma!" Emily's voice came from the kitchen.

"In here." Charlotte added the soap, turned the dial to the normal setting, and closed the top of the washer.

She could hear the stomping of Pete and Bob's boots on the doormat and then the sound of them entering the house.

"Grandma, come quick!" Emily said again.

Charlotte hurried into the kitchen, the tone in Emily's voice causing the tiny hairs on the back of her neck to stand up straight.

A frown filled Emily's face, and she swung the empty egg basket in front of her, her eyes wide. "Grandma, you're not going to believe this. Someone's been in the chicken coop."

"Someone?"

"Yeah, it had to be . . . a person. Because all the eggs are GONE. There wasn't one egg left!"

"And the chickens? Did we lose any?"

"No, the chickens are fine. It was just the eggs."

Bob was washing his hands in the sink. "I bet it's those guys from the combine crew. We let strangers onto our land

and look what's come of it." He turned off the water, but instead of drying his hands on a dishtowel, he shook them out, making splatters on her kitchen window.

Pete pushed his hat back from his face. "C'mon, Dad, you can't be serious. Do you think they'd come back for a few measly eggs? Besides, the thefts in the garden happened *before* the combine crew arrived. What I don't understand is how they got in. I didn't hear Toby barking, did you?"

"No, no barking." Bob shot Charlotte a glance. "That's because the dog's been sleeping with Christopher."

She crossed her arms over her chest. "Just under his bed. It makes him feel better."

"Under his bed, huh? I don't think so. I saw it for myself last night when I went in to check on him. Toby was lying right on Christopher's feet, and she jumped down when she saw me." Bob poured himself a cup of coffee. "That dog's not stupid," he mumbled to no one in particular. "She's a working dog, not a pet. She's gonna get soft."

Bob took a sip of his coffee and then stirred the sausage gravy Charlotte had simmering on the stovetop. Next, he opened the door to check on the biscuits baking inside the oven. A whiff of fresh bread and a blast of hot air filled the kitchen. With a smile, Bob closed the door again.

Then, as if remembering their conversation, he leaned against the counter and crossed his arms, the frown returning.

"But not tonight," Bob grumbled. "Tonight Toby's sleeping outside."

THE REST OF THE DAY was filled with ordinary chores, for which Charlotte was glad. She worked around the house mindlessly, and her brain tried to come up with a logical explanation for the missing vegetables and eggs. There wasn't one. A gentle rain fell outside the window. Sam was working at the computer on the desk across the room, checking e-mail. After a few minutes, he let out a loud sigh of frustration, complaining about the dinosaur computer. Then he headed out the door with his soccer ball. Christopher still had his nose in one of those books.

"Grandma, can you toss me that blanket?" Emily lay on the floor, flipping through the channels on the TV and shivering.

Charlotte snagged the blanket from the back of the sofa and tossed it in Emily's direction. "You cold? Well, I suppose it didn't get this cold in San Diego in September, did it?"

"It didn't get this cold at Christmas!" Emily's teeth clattered.

Charlotte thought about telling her granddaughter that it might help if she put on a sweatshirt over her thin T-shirt and some fuzzy socks on her bare feet, but she didn't dare. That morning, after she noticed Emily's clothes in the laundry were more suited for summer than fall, Charlotte had offered to take Emily clothes shopping.

As she ran out the door to catch the bus, Emily had called back over her shoulder an insistence that her old clothes were fine.

When Charlotte called Melody for advice, Melody gave her counsel similar to what Hannah said about Sam.

"Let it go. When she gets cold enough she'll ask. Put the ball in her court."

In his recliner Bob read his Louis L'Amour novel, and Charlotte was sure he was completely swept away in his fictional world where the young rugged cowboy always saved the day. But then Bob surprised her by rising and moving to the small stove in the corner.

"Emily's right. It's a mite cold around here. What do you think, Ma? How about I light up the corn burner?"

"The what?" Emily sat up to watch.

Bob opened a wooden box by the side of the stove, slid open the compartment in the back of the burner, and filled it with dry corn from the box. Then he took some matches, hunkered down, and lit the pilot light. Within a few seconds, the stove began its work.

"Wow, Grandpa. I didn't know you could use that old thing." Christopher put the book down and eyed the contraption. "I just thought it was one of Grandma's antiques."

"Well, just because something's old doesn't mean it's not useful." Charlotte winked at Bob. "That corn burner was used by your great-grandparents when your grandpa was a boy." She tussled Christopher's hair. "And speaking of boys, I know a young one who needs to head upstairs for his bath."

"Okay." Christopher's shoulders sagged as he turned and headed toward the stairway. "If you say so."

The front door opened, and Charlotte glanced up to see Sam standing in the doorway. "Grandma, can you come here for a second?"

Charlotte rose from her chair and moved to the door.

Sam stood with the soccer ball tucked under his arm and a shy look on his face. She neared, and he leaned in close, whispering in her ear. "Grandma, I don't want to announce it to everyone, but it, uh, smells like beer out here, by the side of the house. I don't know who's been drinking, but I just didn't want you to think it's me."

Charlotte sniffed the air and didn't notice anything out of the ordinary.

"You can't smell it?" Sam raised his eyebrows. "Maybe it's whoever has been getting into the garden and the eggs. Do you think..." His words trailed off. Then his worried gaze met hers. "Why do you think they're coming around? Are we safe?"

She sniffed the air again, this time recognizing the strong smell of the corn-burner stove. Laughter burst from Charlotte's lips.

"That's our stove." She sucked in a breath. "It burns corn, and it just smells like that. It does sort of smell like beer. After all these years I guess I've just gotten used to it."

On the front porch, Pete sat under the eaves with guys from the combine crew who'd come back to talk about the corn harvest. They'd found more work around town and had stayed longer in the area. They were a decent bunch of guys and Charlotte would have invited them to supper, but she felt like she was walking a fine line between being friendly and seeming to Bob like she was taking Pete's side. Already Bob had mentioned more than once that he didn't trust them. More than once he'd also implied they'd had something to do with the garden thefts.

"In the spring there's a new type of seed that I've been hearing about," a stocky man with reddish blond hair said. "Maybe you should consider attending the Nebraska Soybean Day and Machinery Expo. I attended a great work-shop last year on the most common yield-limiting factors in soybean production."

"They even make the best soy doughnuts you can imagine," a thin guy with a long neck commented.

Charlotte stifled a laugh and scrunched her nose at the idea of a soy doughnut. She turned, preparing to return inside the house, when she noticed Bob standing there. He'd overheard the same conversation, but his expression wasn't as jolly.

She stood in front of him, motioning for him to scoot to the side so she could slip by. He did, but just slightly. He crossed his arms over his chest as he peered down at the group of men congregating on the steps.

Noticing for the first time that his parents were there, Pete glanced up. He readjusted his cap. "So, how about those Cornhuskers? Do you think it's going to be a winning season?"

The three men on the steps turned and regarded the two standing in the doorway. They each nodded an acknowledgment and Charlotte waved back.

Charlotte leaned against Bob's shoulder, standing on her tiptoes to whisper in his ear. "Maybe we should shut the door. We just lit the stove, and we're letting all the cold air in."

"Or letting all the hot air out." Bob stepped inside and shut the door harder than he needed to. "And there happens to be a lot of hot air around here."

Charlotte crossed her arms over her chest. "Bob, really, they're just trying to help. Pete's just trying to help."

He nodded once, but she could tell he didn't agree. Instead, he moved past her and fed more dry corn into the corn burner.

Then Bob sat down again and picked up his novel, seeking escape, it seemed from the world around him. Charlotte felt another chill come over her. She grabbed a quilt that was folded up next to the couch, sat down, and tucked it around her. Her eyes grew heavy with the sounds of *Fresh Prince of Bel-Air* playing on the television. Usually she couldn't sleep with so much going through her head, but as she sat there she felt her eyes growing heavy.

She didn't know if she'd drifted off for two minutes or twenty, but when she opened her eyes, Christopher was sauntering down the stairs pink and fresh and dewy from his bath. Sam sat in front of the corn burner with that old hand-held video game that Pete had picked up at a yard sale a couple of weeks ago. And Emily now sat on the couch, blanket wrapped around her, watching a *Family Feud* rerun with the volume so low that Charlotte wasn't sure how the girl could hear it. Every now and then laughter burst from Emily's lips. Her head threw back and her shoulders shook. Yet not all was peaceful. Even with the contented appearance of the children, Bob's firm grasp on the edges of his novel told her that family feuds weren't limited to TV game shows.

She rubbed her hands together, deciding to insert some fun into the evening. "I've got an idea. How about some hot chocolate?"

"I'll help!" Christopher ran to the pantry, bringing out the large canister of cocoa. He then moved to the fridge and pulled out the milk.

Charlotte's mind took her back to another blonde child just his size. She saw glimpses of Denise in the slight turn of Christopher's nose and the way he swept the tip of his tongue around his lips when he was concentrating. In this case, he was focused on getting out a pan without causing the others to tumble from the cabinet.

She knelt down and helped him, shutting the cabinet as he hurried to the counter and the milk jug.

"Christopher, why don't you just heat the milk in the microwave? It might be easier."

"I dunno." He shrugged as the milk glugged into the pan. "This is the way my mom always did it."

"You're right. That *is* the way she always did it. I forgot about that. Your grandpa taught her that."

"Grandpa? Really?"

Charlotte glanced over and noticed Bob had laid aside his book. He too was watching Christopher spoon the powder into the milk and swirl it around in the pan, pausing only to turn up the temperature on the stovetop.

She noticed a rim of tears in Bob's eyes and imagined he was remembering back, pulling out memories like he'd tugged out the plentiful weeds that had threatened her fall mums.

Lord, help him. Ease all the hurt deep inside Bob's heart. The loss of Denise. The loss of his health. The loss of consistency in his day.

And, Lord, show me what to do.

Chapter Twenty-Five

S am, can you do me a favor and tell Uncle Pete dinner's on the table?" Charlotte looked out the window,
wondering where the day had gone. Another school
day. Another trip to town. Another pile of laundry freshly
folded and put away. "Where is Pete anyway? I've hardly
seen him all day."

"In his room reading."

"Reading?"

"Yeah, lots of pamphlets and stuff. He's gotten real boring, I'll tell you that." Sam brushed his too-long hair from
his face and continued bouncing his soccer ball from knee
to knee, like Pete used to toss a baseball from hand to hand.
Charlotte had to admit he was quite good with that ball.

"That's odd. Pete's not the reading type," she mumbled,
then chided herself for doing so. *He's a grown man. A man
has a right to read.*

From his place at the dinner table, Bob didn't comment.
She didn't know if he was uptight about Sam's words or
Sam's playing with a ball in the house.

"Wonder what pamphlets he's reading?" she said to no
one in particular. No one answered.

A few minutes later, when Pete entered, he tossed something into the kitchen trash and then sat. He didn't stay quiet long enough for anyone to bring up the subject. Instead, Pete asked Sam about school, and Emily about her weekend plans, and Christopher about his video game scores. They answered, seemingly oblivious to the tension in the air and Pete's nervous blabbering. Bob was just the opposite and didn't speak a word.

Dinner finished, and Bob opened the *Children's Story Bible.*

Bob read about how God commanded Moses to throw a stick into the water. Moses did, and the water turned sweet.

Wish we could turn a few bitter things sweet around here, Charlotte thought.

Bob closed the book, and Christopher's mouth dropped open. "Was that a magic stick?" Christopher asked.

"No, more like a powerful God," Bob answered.

"Didn't they just cross the Red Sea?" Emily asked. "God just saved them—you'd think they'd be a little more grateful."

"You'd think?" Sam rose and grabbed his plate off the table. Then he glanced back at his grandfather. "We're excused, right?"

"Yes, Sam, you're excused." Bob leaned back in his chair.

Instead of dispersing all over the house, Emily cleared the dishes, and Sam joined in. Charlotte wondered if their helpfulness had anything to do with the Bible story.

Even Bob helped. He cleared the serving bowl, with a few green beans clinging to the side. He carried the bowl to the trash, scraping the beans in, and then he paused, focusing on something in the trash.

When he turned around, his eyes were narrowed into a

glare, and he stared at Pete as if shooting fiery darts his direction.

Sam must have noticed the look too. He sidled up to his grandpa. "Why don't you and Grandma take another walk, like the other night?" Sam's tone was too kind and too cheerful.

Charlotte sauntered over to Bob. "What do you think? Care for a stroll?"

Bob shrugged. "Actually, you mentioned earlier that we're low on some things, like bread and lunch meat. I was hoping you could run to town with the kids and pick up the groceries."

"Tonight?" She glanced at the clock in the kitchen. "But the store closes in an hour."

Bob's lips pressed into a thin line, and she knew he really needed to talk to Pete alone.

Instead, Charlotte ignored the dirty dishes piled in the sink and clapped her hands together. "Actually, kids, the dishes can wait. Why don't we go get some groceries and then stop at Mel's for a treat?"

Two minutes later, when they walked to the car, she could see Pete and Bob through the kitchen window. As she expected, their "discussion" had already begun—and from the looks of the way Bob's arms were swinging as he talked, she knew that it was going to be a long one. Thank goodness for Mel's. A bright cheery place and something super sweet and gooey were just what she needed.

BY THE TIME THEY GOT HOME, the moon was hanging like a large silver dollar in the velvet sky, casting a peaceful glow over the farm. As soon as she climbed out of her car, Charlotte knew there was trouble.

In town, she'd picked up the few groceries and then discovered Mel's was already closed, due to a private birthday gathering inside. The trip was shorter than she anticipated —too soon for the "discussion" to have ended. Bob's voice could be heard even from outside, followed by Pete's.

Leaving the groceries in the car and motioning for the kids to stay put, she hurried inside. She entered, letting the screen door slam behind her, but neither Bob nor Pete seemed to notice she was there.

"Have you planned the funeral, Pete? Because the way you're acting, it seems like you think I'm done and buried," Bob shouted.

"What are you talking about? We went over this already." Pete slammed his fist on the counter. "I'm trying to make sure that *doesn't* happen. If I don't step in, you're gonna work *yourself* to death. Is that what you want? Do we need two funerals in one year? Do you want to leave Mom to raise these kids on her own?"

"What kind of question is that? So you think you know better than me how to take care of this farm? How to take care of myself? You didn't even finish—"

"Bob! Please." Charlotte stepped forward and lifted her hands, refusing to let him go down the path this conversation was heading.

She turned to Pete, pointing a finger at his nose. "And you? Do you remember what the word *respect* means?"

Pete pushed out his chest. "Yeah, and respect goes both ways."

"Yes, you're right." She peered at Bob. In all their years together she could count on one hand the number of times he'd acted this way, but most of them involved Pete. The two had always butted heads, mostly due to the fact that Pete was more like his father than either would admit.

"Surely there is nothing more important than love for family. Nothing." She willed her voice to calm. "Now, what's the reason for this hollering?"

Bob pointed to the trash can. Charlotte made her way over and saw a stack of farming brochures under a splatter of grease and a few green beans.

"And what is it I'm lookin' at?" She glanced to Pete for an explanation.

Pete readjusted his cap. "Well, this has been a good farm, a productive farm for many years. From Dad's great-grandpa on down. We've counted on it producing, and it's done well. But you just have to wonder how long it can keep up. Why, Marshall . . ."

Bob grunted.

"Marshall?" Charlotte asked.

"Yeah, one of the guys I met in the combine crew. He travels all around and helps farmers at harvest. He was telling me what some other farmers—"

"*Other* farmers on *other* kinds of land. How does he know what will work here—"

"Bob, please, you're not giving him a chance to share his side of the story."

"It's just that I was looking into some new methods, maybe some new seed. Nothing's set in stone. I'm just try-ing to find a way to make the farm more efficient. I worry the land won't be able to continue being cultivated, fertilized, even irrigated the same and still be productive." Pete stroked his chin. "And it's not just what Marshall says. I've been reading the paper. Older farms aren't able to make working the land worthwhile. Farmers are retiring. Farms are shutting down. The young people are moving away to bigger cities. And towns just like Bedford are turning into ghost towns."

Instead of commenting, Bob moved toward the sink and leaned forward against its rim, taking in the moonlit view outside the window. Charlotte watched as his shoulders rose and fell, rose and fell.

She also guessed that with his breaths, he was sending out a few desperate prayers as well.

"But I haven't done anything wrong," Pete continued. "I'm just doing some research. I haven't acted ... I just wanted to see what else is out there, getting ideas."

"Just like you did with the combine crew?" Bob's tone was even, but Charlotte could still hear the snip in his voice.

"That was different. I knew you'd argue. I knew you would work day and night to fix your old combine and wear yourself out even before you got to the fields. I had to weigh the options. I knew you'd be mad, but I figured it was better than the alternative."

Neither spoke for a few long minutes. Charlotte could hear the kids outside, walking around the farm and making sure all the doors and pens were latched and secure for the night—doing Pete's normal chores without even being asked.

Charlotte moved to the dining room and sat. Pete

followed, plunking down into a chair at the other end of the table. From her view, she could still see Bob staring out the window. Now the only sound was the ticking of the old clock on the wall and the sound of Toby scratching at the door, wanting in.

"Never used to do that," Bob commented.

"Well, I was never forced to make these decisions before. All the stakes rose with the kids here now. I—"

"That's not what I'm talking about," Bob interrupted. "Toby. When did she start that scratchin' to be let in? She's not made to be a house dog."

Surprised laughter burst from Pete's lips.

"I guess a lot of things are changing around here," Charlotte said. "I think we're all trying to figure out how things work."

Pete rose, strode back into the kitchen, and poured a cup of decaf coffee that Charlotte had brewed for them to enjoy after dinner. Then, glancing at his dad, Pete reached into the cupboard and pulled down another cup. He got the milk out of the refrigerator and added a splash into each mug, handing one to his father.

Charlotte waited as they sipped from their blue mugs, glancing at them to make sure the fight was over, or at least paused for the time being.

She rose. "Guess I'll get the things out of the car." Neither followed.

The boys were waiting outside, sitting on the steps. Emily was curled up in the car, shivering in her skirt and T-shirt. *A whole mess of stubborn people 'round here*, she thought, spying her granddaughter.

Charlotte and Christopher each grabbed a bag of groceries, and Sam grabbed two. And when they entered their house, with their arms laden down with groceries, Bob and Pete still stood at the same place—shoulder to shoulder, leaning against the counter. The same set of the jaw. The same pensive gazes. The same slow sips from their coffee cups.

As she placed a couple of loaves in the bread box, Bob grunted and took a few of the pamphlets out of the trash, brushing them off and stalking away.

Chapter
Twenty-Six

On Thursday afternoon the kids hadn't been off the bus five minutes when Christopher hurried into the house and found Bob reading over the agricultural reports.

He rushed right past Charlotte and the pile of socks she was sorting. He stopped before Bob's chair. "Grandpa, there's something I want to show you."

Bob peered over the top of his reading glasses.

"Now's as good a time as any, I suppose."

Christopher lifted his hands in front of his grandpa. "Okay, stay right there."

Bob chuckled as Christopher ran out the door.

Charlotte glanced up from the pile of socks.

"I wonder what he found this time," Bob mused.

Charlotte found a pair of Sam's socks in the pile and folded them together. "You've got me. That kid is always finding something. Yesterday it was chicken feathers and wire cutters. Today it was nails and matches . . . even a piece of chewed-up gum in a wrapper. Can you imagine what a mess that would be if that went through the wash?"

A few minutes later Christopher returned with an old,

rusty, dirty hunk of metal that looked like some type of machine part. Charlotte bit her tongue as she noticed how he pressed the dirty thing against his shirt.

"Do you know what this is?" Christopher asked.

Bob took the piece and turned it over in his hands. A look of wonder came over his face.

Charlotte's hands stilled and her brow furrowed, surprised by his reaction.

Finally, he released a long breath.

"Yeah, I know what it is. It's a carburetor."

"Yes!" Christopher punched his arm out, then pulled it back, tucking his elbow next to his ribs. "I got it right."

"You figured it out?"

"Uh-huh, in one of the old books that I got at the library." He moved to the stairs and paused. Then he turned and hurried to the back porch instead. Charlotte's eyes widened as he brought in a library book. It was dirty, with a torn page, and the edges of all the pages were slightly curled from the moisture of the recent rain.

Charlotte stopped herself from exclaiming over the condition of the book. *I wonder how much the library is going to charge to replace this?*

"See!" Christopher pointed to an illustration. It showed details of the side view of a motor.

"You're right. You figured it out." Bob looked closer at the book. "This photo is from a Ford, but I think your carburetor is actually from an automobile named Diana, from the Moon Motor Car Company."

Christopher's eyes widened. "Then it *is* from outer space?" His lips rounded into a circle. "Whoa."

Bob's boisterous laughter shook the room. "Not quite. It

was the name of the car company—not the location of it. In fact, I think I have an old car manual from that vehicle somewhere around here."

"Can you show me?"

Bob nodded and Charlotte could see a twinkle of excitement in his eyes.

"What does it do? You know, the carburetor? Does it make cars go super fast?"

"Actually, it makes them *go*. Today, new cars use something called fuel injection that shoots just the right amount of fuel into the engine, but most other things around the farm have carburetors, like mowers and chainsaws."

"And old cars did too?"

"Yep, you're a quick learner."

"So how does it work?" Christopher scratched his head.

Bob held it out for Christopher to get a better look. "Well, the carburetor mixes just the right amount of gasoline with the air so the engine runs properly. If there isn't enough fuel mixed with the air the engine runs lean and that will damage the engine."

"Sort of like when I forget to eat breakfast? My mom used to say that it wasn't good, 'cause I wouldn't get enough fuel for my body." Christopher smiled. "That's like running lean, right?"

"Your mom was smart." Bob chocked Christopher's chin with a knuckle. "Must be where you got it."

"Yeah."

Charlotte noticed some of the twinkle disappear from Christopher's gaze as Bob mentioned his mom. Bob must have noticed it too because he quickly turned his attention back to the machine part in his hand.

"So, my half-pint archeologist. Where did you find this?"

Christopher pointed to the meadow beyond the window. "Out there. Come on, I'll show you."

Charlotte watched as Bob rose and winked at her. "Grandma, you care to join us?"

A dozen reasons not to, a dozen chores, flashed into her mind. She had chores to do, but now she was curious about that old car part. Besides, her heart warmed as she noticed Bob and Christopher standing side by side.

"All right. You win. Let me get my shoes."

The evening light had already begun to fade as they sauntered outside. As she walked down the porch steps with Toby at her side, she noticed Pete had finished up the milking for the evening and was heading back to his apartment. Charlotte waved, and he tipped his hat back.

They moved toward the meadow. To the right of them, tall stalks of corn trembled in the evening breeze, as if they'd all gotten a case of stage fright.

"So, is it important? Did I find an antique?" Christopher asked, his small tennis shoes sinking slightly into the soft ground as he bounced at Bob's side.

"I don't know if it's the type of antique that Grandma would put up in the house, but it sure is a piece of family history. In fact, this piece of history takes us back to the 1930s when there was something called the Dust Bowl crisis."

"Dust Bowl?" Christopher plucked a strand of grass and examined it as he walked.

"Yes, it was a hard time for our country. It was a time when there was little rain and nothing grew. Farms all over turned to fields of dust, and there wasn't anything anyone could do."

"Not fields of dust, *bowls* of dust," Christopher corrected.

"Yes, and my father, your great-grandpa, was only a teenager then. And like most people, our family wondered if they could hold on. They prayed they'd be able to stay strong until rain came again."

"Did rain come?"

"Eventually, but not for a very long time. For months and months they trusted God's provision and stayed on the farm. Stevensons were tough back then, that's for sure."

As she listened to Bob's words, Charlotte glanced around at their bountiful fields. The soybeans had been harvested in record time. The corn harvest would soon begin. Though the bank account wasn't bulging, they had enough.

Thank You, Lord. She silently prayed as they strolled along. *Thank You for reminding me . . .*

Christopher pointed to an area just ahead featuring a large oak tree. "Right here. This is where I found it."

Bob hunkered down and scooped up a handful of soil, allowing it to filter through his fingers. He stared intently at the dirt as if reading a story in each speck.

"One day, my grandma, your great-*great*-grandma, heard a knock at the door," he began. "It was a man whose car had broken down. The man had a woman and baby with him— all were painfully thin. The man didn't ask for much. In fact, he only asked for one thing."

"What was that?" Christopher asked. "A job? A place to live?"

"No, son. He only asked if they could spare food for his sick baby."

"Land's sakes. I couldn't imagine." Charlotte clutched her arms to her. An aching filled her gut as she tried to imagine being in such a spot.

"My family—our family—took in this hungry couple. We fed them. Our family didn't have much, but they had enough to share."

"Did the baby get better?" Christopher cradled the carburetor as if clinging to the infant himself.

Bob sighed. "Unfortunately not. He never gained his strength back and died on the farm. Eventually Grandpa William and Great-Grandma Betty helped the couple get a new part for their car. They threw the old one on the farm's dump and the sad family went on their way. They never heard from them again. But that sick baby, and that desperate family, so touched my great-grandparents, they vowed from that day on to make Heather Creek Farm a place of refuge for all who needed help."

"Refuge?" Christopher scratched his head near the blond cowlick that always stuck up no matter how many times he combed it.

"A place of safety. Where you go to be cared for and looked after," Charlotte answered.

The sun slipped over the horizon and the last orange rays stretched toward them, as if not quite willing to slip away.

Charlotte took Christopher's free hand. "We better get back. It's getting dark."

As they headed back, Charlotte smiled to herself at the sight of the house, the warm glow from the windows.

"Were there other times?" Christopher's words interrupted her thoughts. "You know, when we helped other people on this farm?"

"Actually, yes, when I was just a tot I remember my mom having a Victory Garden," Bob answered.

"A what?"

"It was during World War II," Charlotte added. "Most of the men were off at war. People put gardens wherever they could find space—in backyards, on rooftops. Farms not only had to provide food for their own families and the people stateside, but also for our troops overseas. So most women had huge gardens, much bigger than the one I have today."

Bob held out his hand, and Christopher placed the carburetor in it. "And while the food supply did help, it also made people feel good—as if they were doing their part. They learned the truth of what the Bible talks about—that it's better to give than to receive."

They neared the porch, but Bob paused before heading up the steps. "Of course, there have been other times—more recent times." Bob glanced in Charlotte's direction. "It seems like your grandma is always baking up something special to take to a sick person in our community. Or digging through my work shirts to share with a family in need. From the time we were first married, your grandma has been a fine example of reaching out to others as God would."

Christopher gently took the carburetor from his grandfather's hands. "Then I think you should have it, Grandma. A special antique, just for you!"

Warmth filled her chest, and she accepted it with a smile. "Thank you, Christopher. I'm sure Grandpa will help me find the perfect place for it." She squatted down so her face was level with his. "And you're right. It's very special indeed."

THE NEXT DAY WAS FRIDAY and another teacher in-service day, so the kids were home. They didn't seem to mind though, especially Christopher. From the moment he woke up, he and Bob were inseparable.

After breakfast, they headed out to the place where they found the carburetor, to dig around to see if there was any other treasure out there. Sam was off with Pete checking the fence in the far quarters, and Emily had been invited to spend the day in Harding with Bill's wife, Anna, and the girls. Before they headed out the door, Charlotte had slipped a fifty-dollar bill to Anna.

"If you see anything warm and appropriate, something that Emily likes, can you get it?"

"Of course," Anna had said. "You know how I love shopping."

The house was empty now, and though Charlotte thought it was great that relationships were deepening among the family members, when she looked around the kitchen, overwhelming feelings popped up like unwanted weeds in her garden.

Dishes teetered in a stack in the sink, and she was sure the only thing keeping them from tumbling to the kitchen floor was the food that had dried on them, sticking them together like glue. On the countertop closest to the door was a pile of mail mixed with school books, important notes from teachers, and school schedules. Somewhere underneath was a book Melody had lent her on raising teenagers in this day and age.

"If only I had a break from the teenagers to read it," Charlotte muttered under her breath.

Charlotte weighed her options. Dishes or paperwork? After glancing back and forth, back and forth between the two stacks, she finally settled on paperwork, especially the bills. Missed payments meant more interest, something they couldn't take on.

She separated the school books from the bills. Biology, Sam. Earth science, Emily. *Our Fifty States*, Christopher. Charlotte stacked the books into individual piles, one for each of the kids, telling herself to look for wicker baskets at the fabric store so they could organize their own stuff.

As she restacked the books, she noticed a bright pink sheet of paper poking out from inside of Emily's earth science book.

IMPORTANT REMINDER: Your region and climate report is due THIS Monday. The assignment will be docked one letter grade for every day it is late.

Region and climate report? Charlotte searched her brain trying to remember if Emily had mentioned the report, or if she'd even brought home one research book.

"Oh, that girl," she mumbled under her breath.

Charlotte picked up the cordless phone and dialed Anna's cell phone. Thankfully, Harding got better service than Bedford and the call went straight through.

"Hello?"

"Hi, Anna, this is Mom. Can I talk to Emily?"

"Sure, hold on."

She could hear the mumbling of voices and the sound of car noises. A few seconds later Emily's voice came over the phone.

"Hello?"

"Hi, it's Grandma."

"Yeah?"

"I was just cleaning the kitchen, and I was straightening your books, and I noticed you have a report due Monday."

"Yeah, so?"

"So when were you going to tell me about this?"

"Um, before Monday."

"And did you plan on a trip to the library? Or did you check to see if we even have ink for the printer? I don't want to be on the Internet until two o'clock Monday morning trying to help you . . ."

"*Grandma . . .*"

". . . find the information you need. In fact, maybe you going to Harding today wasn't such a great idea."

From out the window Charlotte spotted Bob and Christopher heading back to the house. Bob held something in his hand.

"Grandma . . ." Emily's voice raised an octave.

"Yeah?"

"I talked to my teacher. She says I can do my report about the climate of San Diego, you know, just talk about the weather, the types of plants, the Santa Ana winds—stuff I'm familiar with." In the background Charlotte could hear Anna's girls arguing about something and their mother trying to calm them down.

"I just need to go through my photo album and find some photos of the beach and stuff. I have a lot that I took last year."

Emily's voice was patient, speaking to Charlotte as if she were the child.

"Oh, okay." Charlotte took a deep breath. "I guess I should have known you had it under control, Emily. Sorry to bother you, honey. Have a great time."

Charlotte hung up the phone and leaned on the counter, pressing her face into her hands.

AFTER SHE FINISHED with the bills, Charlotte hauled up four boxes of canning jars from the basement, sneezing five times in a row from the dust that tickled her nose. Just as she set the last box in the kitchen and filled the sink with warm, sudsy water, Bob and Christopher entered the house. Charlotte noted tears in Christopher's eyes as he pointed to the cross in his grandfather's hand.

"Look what we found, Grandma. Near the spot where I found the carburetor."

A pang of heartache tugged at Charlotte's heart as she realized the cross must have some connection to the sick baby who'd stopped by the farm during the Dust Bowl.

Without another word, Bob and Christopher moved to the dining room and settled into the chairs. From the far-off looks in their eyes and their melancholy manner, it appeared as if they'd made the connection too.

Although she was busy washing her canning jars, thinking about how far behind she was in getting the produce put up, she kept her ears attuned to Bob and Christopher, wondering if either of them would decide to talk about it.

The sink full of dishwater was sudsy and warm, and it calmed her despite Bob's and Christopher's mournful looks.

The minutes ticked by on the old grandfather clock. Finally, Christopher spoke. "Do you think, Grandpa, that's where they buried the baby?"

Bob shrugged. "I'm not sure. It could have been . . . or maybe it was just a memorial marker—a symbol to represent the loss of the baby's life."

"It sort of reminds me of my mom. We put a cross on her grave too." Christopher lowered his head, and Charlotte noted his shoulders trembling. She knew she should say something, but didn't know what. Christopher had come so far, and she hated the thought that he'd slip back into the quiet and skittish shell of a boy he'd been when the children had first come to the farm.

"It's strange to think that if that baby had lived, he'd be an old man by now. In his seventies at least," Charlotte said from the kitchen, hoping Bob didn't mind her butting in.

"Is that older than grandpa?" Christopher's hand reached out and touched the cross that someone, years ago, had carved out of wood.

Bob chuckled slightly. "Yes, a few years older than me."

"Do you think God helped that family?" Christopher drummed his fingers on the *Children's Story Bible* sitting at the table. "I mean, God was with those Israel people a long time ago. Maybe he was with that family too."

"I have a feeling he was, because your great-great-grandparents weren't just kind men and women. They did what they did because they believed in God. It was God's kindness that came out of them." Bob handed the cross to Christopher.

"God's kindness? That's cool." Christopher stood and hurried into the kitchen. He held it out to Charlotte. "Grandma, I know you most likely don't want to put that carburetor in the kitchen, but what about this?" He held out the cross.

"Yes, I think I can find a perfect spot for this." She took the cross from him. It wasn't much bigger than her hand, yet under the layer of dirt, the wood was smooth.

"Why don't I clean it up and set it in the kitchen window?"

Bob followed Christopher into the kitchen. "I have that old brochure for that car around here somewhere. Do you want to help me look? I think it's out in the tractor shed in one of my drawers."

"Sure, Grandpa." Without another word Christopher darted out the door.

A twinkle lit Bob's eyes, and he followed.

Charlotte turned back to the sink and took out a moist sponge. With gentle strokes she wiped the dirt off of the cross. She tried to imagine all the years it had lain hidden in the ground, under the green pasture grass of spring and summer. Under a layer of dirt and fall leaves. Inside the frozen ground during winter. Yet, now found years later, the message of hope was still the same. It hadn't changed through all life's changes.

When the cross was finally clean, she moved the red and white teacup she'd gotten for Valentine's Day years ago out of the windowsill, and replaced it with the cross—propping it in the corner so it would stand up.

She cocked her head, looking toward the barn to see if Pete and Sam were still out there and considering what they would think about Christopher's discovery.

Charlotte finished rinsing the canning jars and lined them up on a dishtowel on the counter to dry. Then she glanced at the cross again. It was a gentle reminder that God had loved and cared for those at Heather Creek Farm for many years. He would continue to do so for many more years—even when these children were older, and even when this generation passed away. Even then God wouldn't leave. No matter what.

Chapter
Twenty-Seven

Sam's face seemed to be only inches from the cereal bowl as he scooped sugary flakes into his mouth. He was back from checking fence with Pete and since it wasn't quite lunch time, he'd discovered a second breakfast was a good solution for his growling stomach.

Charlotte was in the kitchen parboiling a flat of peaches she'd picked up at the store, with plans to spend the afternoon canning those and the green beans she'd harvested in the garden. More produce had been missing this morning. They would have to figure out what was tearing up this garden soon, or there would be nothing left.

"Whas dis?" Sam said with a mouthful of cereal. He finished chewing and swallowed. Then he lifted the faded orange booklet from the dining room table and waved it in Charlotte's direction.

"It's a booklet your grandpa found this morning. Your great-grandfather must have received it when he ordered a part for a car he fixed a long time ago. I told Grandpa to leave it there. I thought you'd find it interesting."

"Oh yeah, Christopher showed me that old carburetor. So Grandpa figured out what it was for?"

"Yes, he did. You should ask him about it. It's a pretty interesting story. Maybe you'd find it interesting for your report."

Sam nodded but didn't comment about the report. He read the brochure, chuckling to himself. "No way . . . this is a manual for an old car called the Diana. Listen to this . . ." Sam cleared his throat and lowered his voice. "'It is important that during the first one thousand miles a speed of twenty-five miles an hour is not exceeded.' Can you believe that? Uncle Pete's old tractor moves faster than that! Man, that would have taken forever just to get from here to Bedford."

Sam exited, meeting her gaze, and motioned to the barn with a jerk of his chin.

"In a minute," she mouthed and then pointed to the large pot on the stove.

Earlier, he'd reported that he and Pete were up to something —a big something in the barn. Something they wanted her to come look at. But that would have to wait. The peaches looked almost ready. She slid a tine of a fork under the skin on one and it came off easily. She placed the fork on the counter and then turned down the heat on the burner.

Bob approached, glancing into the pot. "Doing anything today?"

"Doing anything?" She turned to him and placed her hand on her hip. "I have a million things to do. Why?"

"Never mind."

"What, Bob?"

"I was just thinking of straightening up the cellar."

"Today?"

"Sure, it needs to get done."

Charlotte could tell from the look in his eyes that he wasn't just commenting. He was asking for her help. Help she couldn't give.

"I wish I could join you. It's just there are so many other things." She thought about listing them, but she already noted the disappointed look in Bob's gaze. Before the kids came they'd always worked together on projects. Sometimes they talked while they worked, but Charlotte knew Bob enjoyed just having her there.

Bob shrugged and moved to the cellar door. His shoulders sagged and a cloak of guilt draped over Charlotte's shoulders.

"No, wait, I can help." She sighed. "Just give me a few minutes to peel the skins from these peaches, and then I'll be right down."

A smile filled Bob's face, and he moved to the door of the cellar with a lighter step.

Another thing to do. Another person to help.

Lord, if one more person asks one more thing . . . why, I think I'm going to scream.

AS CHARLOTTE SETTLED DOWN with her embroidery project in hand, and some mindless game show blaring out of the TV in the background, Emily announced they should set one final trap for whoever or whatever was getting in the garden. Charlotte reluctantly agreed.

Even though they'd trapped an unwilling victim with their previous attempt, Emily did a better job of informing everyone of the location of the traps this time. She again strung twine and old cans around the perimeter of the garden and the chicken coop.

Charlotte put down her embroidery, and she helped Emily and Christopher set up their bedding in the living room, their Plan B stakeout location.

Sam didn't offer to join them. Instead, he slinked off to his room, and Charlotte guessed that he felt it safer for everyone if he wasn't involved.

Emily curled up on the couch under a multicolored afghan Bob's mother had made thirty-two years ago as a Christmas present for Charlotte after Pete's birth. Christopher lay on the floor between some old blankets, with Toby curled at his feet.

"Sorry, girl, you're gonna have to sleep outside tonight." Charlotte scratched behind the dog's ear.

As if understanding, Toby followed Charlotte to the kitchen, slipped through the door when Charlotte opened it, and trotted down to her doghouse to the right of the porch.

Then Charlotte turned off the lights in the kitchen, imagining the soft warmth of her bed.

She prayed with the kids and then read a chapter out of Christopher's storybook, but when she bid them goodnight, it was Emily who took Charlotte's hand and held on.

"Grandma, can you stay up with us for just a little while?"

"Stay up? I'm not a youngster anymore." Charlotte's back ached, shoulders ached, feet ached. There was a reason why women had babies when they were young. The daily pace was getting to her, and she'd felt she'd aged ten years in the last few months.

She slid her hand from Emily's. "Maybe another time—

when you give me advance warning first. Give me a chance to store up some energy."

Charlotte's eyelids felt heavy, but as she looked down at Emily's sad face, she had a flashback of Denise at that age. While the boys usually fell asleep as soon as their heads hit the pillows, it was Denise who had often wanted to chat, launching into deep topics just as Charlotte was ready to hit the hay for the night. More times than not, she'd promised Denise they'd talk the next day, but usually that didn't happen. Charlotte realized that this time she had another chance. She would always have regrets, but at least she was given the opportunity not to have them twice.

Letting out a heavy sigh, she reached for Emily's hand again and squeezed. "Then again, I suppose I won't be any younger tomorrow. I can stay up for just a little while."

A smile filled Emily's face. "Thanks, Grandma."

Charlotte made herself a cup of tea and then curled up in Bob's chair, flipping through one of her cooking magazines as she tried to think of a meaningful conversation starter.

Emily snuggled on the couch, half sitting and half lying, with her pillow tucked under her arms. Christopher lay on his back with Chewbacca in his hand. The furry stuffed animal jumped and flew through the air, acting out whatever sci-fi storyline happened to be playing through the boy's mind.

"So, Emily, did you get anything in town today?" Charlotte asked, attempting to stifle a yawn.

"Oh yeah, but I had to borrow some money from Aunt Anna. She said it was okay if you paid her back next week or whenever."

Charlotte paused her flipping of the magazine pages. "But I gave her fifty dollars."

"I know, she told me. But the sweatshirt cost more than that."

"Sweatshirt... as in *one*?"

"Yeah, it's from Duo—it's one of my favorite brands."

"You spent fifty dollars on *one* sweatshirt?"

Emily glanced up surprised, as if she finally understood what Charlotte was asking. "Uh, actually, it was seventy-nine dollars. You owe Aunt Anna the other twenty-nine. But it's really cute. You want to see?"

Charlotte could see the excitement in the girl's eyes. But didn't Emily have any idea how hard it was to justify spending that much money on one piece of clothing?

Charlotte's teeth ground together as she tried to hold back harsh comments. Mostly she felt anger simmering right below the surface, and not at Emily. Anna should have known better. Anna might have the money to spend dressing up her girls like two little dolls, but she didn't need to do the same with Emily—especially with Charlotte's money.

"Sure." Charlotte put down her magazine. "Show me what you got." Emily hurried over to a shopping bag tossed on the floor by the bottom of the stairs. She pulled out a gray sweatshirt and slid it on over her pajama top, zipping it up halfway.

"See, isn't it cute?" Emily did a little twirl in front of Charlotte. The gray hoodie wasn't thick like the Carhartt ones Pete and Bob wore. Instead, it was more like a long-sleeved T-shirt with a zipper front and a hood. It had some Chinese symbol on the front that looked as if it had been spray-painted on. It wasn't colorful or exciting, and hardly worth seventy-nine dollars.

"Good thing you told me it was yours. I would have thought it was something Pete picked up at one of his garage sales."

Emily's mouth dropped open. A look of shock flashed in her eyes, quickly followed by a downcast expression.

It was the cappuccino moment all over again. The same hurt feelings—the same misunderstanding. Without a word, Emily slowly unzipped the jacket. With each inch of the zipper, Charlotte felt Emily building a wall around herself, creating a barrier that hadn't been there moments before. Charlotte sat straighter in her chair, determined not to let the wall cement, knowing it would be hard to try to tear it down later.

"Duo, I've never heard of that brand before. It must be a California thing, right?"

"Yeah, a lot of my friends back home wore stuff like this," Emily answered tentatively.

Charlotte pointed to the sweatshirt. "And what does that symbol mean?"

Emily took off the sweatshirt and looked at the symbol closer. "It doesn't mean anything. It's just a symbol."

"Well, symbols usually mean something. It looks like it's some kind of Chinese word." Charlotte shrugged and tried to make her tone as nonchalant as possible. "I don't know. Maybe it's just me, but I'd be wary of wearing something if I didn't know what it meant."

"I bet we can find a book at the library to find out what it means," Christopher said. His head was nestled deep in his pillow and his eyes were closed. If it weren't for the fact his response made sense, Charlotte would have thought he was talking in his sleep.

"Whatever. Books are lame." Emily returned her sweatshirt to the bag, flipped off the living room lights, and settled into her sleeping bag. The room was dark except for the soft glow from the corn burner. Charlotte sipped her tea, trying to think of something to say. She was just about to take her teacup into the kitchen and head to bed herself when Toby's sharp barking split the air. It was quickly followed by a man's shouting . . . not Pete's voice, but someone else's. Older. Unrecognizable. Scared.

Charlotte knew she had to get Bob to call for Pete, but before she even stood, Sam rushed down the stairs and out the door, fully dressed.

"Sam, no wait!"

"Bob!" she yelled, hurrying to their room, ignoring the frightened faces of Emily and Christopher. "Bob, wake up! Come quick!"

Chapter Twenty-Eight

Bob ordered Emily and Christopher to stay in the house with the doors locked. Sam had already run outside, but they didn't argue.

Charlotte insisted on coming too. Bob grabbed his hunting rifle, and together they hurried outside.

Toby's barking had died down, and when Bob and Charlotte rounded the back side of the house, Charlotte could see two flashlights fixed on a figure in the distance. As they neared the garden, she noticed a tall, thin man talking to Pete and Sam. He carried what looked like two plastic sacks in his hands.

The man was older. His clothes were tattered and dirty. He wore a bushy beard and his hair was long. From the looks of it, he hadn't showered in months.

"I didn't mean no harm," the man was saying. "Came to make things right."

"Yeah, well, I'm not sure I believe that, but you're gonna have to talk to my parents. They're the ones you were stealing from." Pete's voice was firm.

Pete glanced back as Bob and Charlotte approached. "Here they come now."

202

Charlotte pulled her bathrobe tight around her, realizing her intuition had been right. It was *someone* who had been stealing from them. The thought of this stranger walking onto their property, taking their things, caused a cold chill to run down her spine. She felt violated, and more than anything she wanted to turn and hurry back to the safety of the house.

The man held out both of the plastic grocery sacks. He shyly glanced up at Bob. "It's not as good as garden-grown, but I met a lady in town who hired me to help her by doing handyman stuff. She paid a little, and I wish I could buy more . . . but it's all I have."

"You're bringing this to us?" Bob scratched his gray hair that was sticking up in all directions from his sleep.

"Did you suddenly grow a conscience?" Pete pointed a finger at the man's chest. "Did you *really* come back to try to make things right?" He took a step closer to the man. "You scared the kids, you know. And I almost got my head knocked off because of you."

"You don't understand. I . . . wasn't the one who took the things. I found out about what the others done. Like I said, I, I . . . just wanted to make it right."

Pete cocked his head, as if he didn't know what to believe. Charlotte studied the man's face closer. He was old and his face was wrinkled like one of the dried-apple dolls she used to make with her kids.

"It's not what you think," he added again.

Bob rested the barrel of the gun on his shoulder and stood in an easy stance that showed the man he meant him no harm, but his voice was firm. "Well, what is it then?

From what I can see you were trespassing on my property—taking what isn't yours."

"I wasn't taking. I was returning what they took. If you'd just give me a chance to explain." The man lowered to one knee and opened one of the grocery bags.

Charlotte peered down at the carrots, potatoes, celery—still in the plastic grocery-store bags.

"So you were repaying what they took? Who is 'they'?" Pete eyed the man suspiciously.

The man glanced from Charlotte to Pete to Bob and then finally his gaze rested back on hers. Charlotte cocked her head in surprise, noting gentleness there. The man shivered beneath his dirty jacket that hung from his bony shoulders.

"They, well—"

Charlotte raised her hand, interrupting him. "Why don't we let the man explain inside? The last thing I need is for all of us to catch a cold."

A few minutes later they were inside, all huddled around the kitchen. Charlotte spooned homemade applesauce into a bowl. She handed it to the man who sat at the table, trying to ignore his strong odor. "You could have come to us," she said. "If you would have asked, we would have given you food."

"But it wasn't like that . . ." The man ate the applesauce, wiping his mouth with the back of his hand. "I joined up with a group in Lincoln a few months ago, and we've been moving from town to town."

"Like hobos?" Sam asked.

The man chuckled. "If you want to call us that. We're travelers, so to speak."

"So what happened next?" Pete crossed his arms over his chest.

"There were 'bout a half dozen of us. We've found odd jobs here and there, but we didn't always make enough to get by."

The man slid the empty bowl away from him and glanced to Charlotte, a look of appreciation in his gaze. She scooped more applesauce into the bowl as he continued.

"I saw your home from off the road, and it looked friendly. I suggested we stop—to look for work. The others didn't listen. I'm a hard sleeper. One night I dozed off and when I woke up they had sacks of produce. I had a feeling deep in my gut where it come from."

"So you didn't say anything? You didn't ask?" Charlotte offered the second helping of applesauce, and he gladly took it.

"No. I didn't. Another time, they had eggs. I knew I had to stop 'em. But then they headed south and I decided to stay. To make it right." He pointed to the grocery sacks he'd brought inside. His sad smile revealed missing teeth. "I haven't always chosen the best of friends. I'm tired of being dragged down by them."

"What's your name?" Christopher stepped closer and touched the man's hand. Charlotte noticed age spots and wrinkles under a layer of dirt.

"Jefferson."

"Is that a first name or a last one?" Emily asked. She

stood farther back from the others, but there was a caring look on her face that Charlotte didn't expect.

"Truth be told, it's been so many years since I've gone by anything else ... I like Jefferson, just Jefferson."

"Don't you have a family?" Sam asked.

"Nah. I was adopted by an older couple who didn't have other kids. When they passed away I decided that seeing the United States seemed to be the most adventurous thing I could do. Sold most all I had and hit the road. It was great for many years, but ..." He glanced around, looking from face to face. Then he lowered his head. "But it's no way to live."

The man finished his applesauce, and Charlotte took the bowl. She turned and placed it in the kitchen sink, noticing the cross in the window. Warmth came over her—feelings of kindness toward the man—and she knew what she had to do. She turned back around and met Bob's gaze. She noted care there too. Then she approached the man.

"Well, Jefferson, I have a feeling that it wasn't by accident you ended up here on Heather Creek Farm. Your friends sure did give us a fright for a time—mostly because we couldn't figure out what was going on." She searched the man's face for any sign of deception. He seemed nice enough, but still ...

"I was thinking I could set up a bed in the barn," Pete said. Pete met Bob's gaze. Bob, too, eyed Jefferson.

"Not a bad idea. It's warm and dry," Bob said.

"Come on, Jefferson, let's see what we can do." Pete headed out to the barn. Jefferson, Charlotte, and Bob followed them out. Five minutes later he was settled in with some old blankets on the straw.

It was after midnight when Bob and Charlotte closed the barn door and headed back to the house. The night was dark and the air smelled like cuttings and damp ground. Bob's large hand reached over and grabbed Charlotte's smaller one. Charlotte saw that the light was still on in Christopher's room, and she guessed he was in his bed reading again. She'd have to head upstairs and make sure he turned it out and got some sleep. Morning would come before they knew it.

Tomorrow, in addition to getting the kids up and fed, fixing meals, and doing the numerous other chores, she also had to figure out how to get some help for Jefferson. Maybe she'd call the church and the used-clothing store in town. She'd also call her prayer group and ask them to start praying. It seemed there just had to be something they could do to get this poor man a more permanent place to stay, some newer clothes, and maybe a "real" job. Her mind spun with possibilities.

"Deep in thought?" Bob asked as they walked up the porch steps. The moon cast a warm glow over his face.

She squeezed Bob's hand and chuckled. "You know what? I was. He needs so much, and it would be great if we could help. And like I told the kids earlier, I don't think it's by chance that he ended up here."

Bob opened the door for her and motioned for her to enter before him.

"You know what else?" Charlotte chuckled.

"Hmm?" He yawned wide.

"I was completely overwhelmed earlier today. My list of things to do and people to take care of overwhelmed me."

She sighed. "You'd think that having another person to feel responsible for would make things worse. But . . . I actually feel better. Reaching out to Jefferson and knowing that I—we—can make a difference in his life is just what I needed."

"It's strange how that works, isn't it?" Bob lowered his voice as they entered the now-quiet house. "Most days I go to bed with more questions than answers—wondering if we're making good choices for the kids. But I also know that we're doing the right thing. It's a good kind of hard." He locked the door behind him and turned off the kitchen light.

Charlotte paused by the bottom of the stairs. "I'm going to turn off Christopher's light. I'll be right down."

She eased her way up the stairs just in case Christopher had fallen asleep with the light on. Emily's door was open, and she heard the faintest snores coming from the girl's room. But when she went to check on Christopher, he was still wide awake, sitting on the edge of his bed as if waiting for Charlotte to come.

"What are you doing up?"

"Thinking."

"About what?"

"Well, back in San Diego, Sam and I always shared a room. Maybe we should do that again and then Jefferson could sleep in Sam's room."

Charlotte thought about that for a minute.

"I'm not sure if that would be the best thing for Jefferson. You see, he's been on his own a long time. He's used to making his own rules and doing as he pleases. Also, you need to understand that though Jefferson seems like a nice guy, it's always important to be cautious with strangers."

"Is that why Jefferson is sleeping out in the barn?"

"Yes. We can help him, but it doesn't mean we're going to make him a part of our family."

That answer seemed to satisfy Christopher. He nodded once and then climbed under his covers.

Charlotte tucked the covers under his chin and gave him a soft kiss on his forehead. Then she walked to the doorway and turned off the bedroom light. The light from the hallway slanted into his room, making a yellow triangle on the floor.

"Grandma?" Christopher mumbled.

She couldn't see his face, but she turned his direction.

"Was I a stranger when I came here?"

"No, Christopher. You were my grandson. And even though I didn't see you often, you've always been in my thoughts . . . and my prayers."

"Thanks, Grandma." She could hear the hint of a smile in his voice.

He turned over, facing the wall.

"Night, Christopher," she said one last time before heading back down the stairs.

Charlotte's head ached with tiredness, and as she walked down the stairs her limbs protested that they were still moving instead of resting. But deep inside, Charlotte felt God's pleasure. It was hard, but worth it.

Oh, so worth it.

Chapter
Twenty-Nine

Charlotte awoke to voices in the kitchen. The kids' voices and someone else's. A man's voice. The voice was old and scruffy, yet it also hinted of laughter. Then she remembered—Emily's trap and the homeless man, Jefferson.

Though her body begged for more rest, something told her to get up. Her head was foggy and her eyes longed to flutter closed for just five more minutes, but light flooded the room, and she knew she'd already slept too long.

Charlotte glanced at the alarm clock. *Nine o'clock!* She jumped out of bed, disbelief flooding over her. She couldn't remember the last time she'd slept so late. Maybe sometime when she was sick or had the flu, but never on a normal Saturday.

She wondered what time the kids had gotten up. Where were Bob and Pete? Did Bob think it was okay to just let Jefferson hang out in the house without someone there?

As Charlotte dressed, she remembered her talk with Christopher last night, and how she'd reminded him that just because someone appeared kind didn't mean that person was safe. Panic clawed at her gut. There was a stranger in the house, and here she was sleeping in.

She washed her face with a hot washcloth, ran a brush through her short hair, and then followed the sounds of voices. She found the kids, Pete, and Jefferson, standing around the kitchen. Relief flooded over her that her son had enough foresight to delay the morning chores and stick around.

Charlotte paused at the sight of their guest and realized that Pete must have given Jefferson some stuff to clean up with. Pete must have offered his shower too.

Their new friend looked different. So different that her first impression was the man of last night was some type of dream and another stranger stood here now. It was only his voice, as Jefferson talked about growing up during the 1930s and 1940s to four attentive listeners, that told her it was the same man.

Jefferson's hair was combed back from his face. The hair was a dirty gray color and even tucked behind his ears it still fell to his shirt collar. Yet their guest was now clean, and cleanly shaven. Without the beard, the hollowness of his cheeks was even more prominent. Thick wrinkles on his forehead told of the hard conditions he'd lived as a "traveler." Yet laugh lines around his eyes proved he had not been totally hardened by his journey.

Pete's jeans and old flannel shirt were improvements from Jefferson's previous clothes. The pants were cinched with a belt, and the denim almost looked pleated the way it bunched together at his waist. The pant's cuffs had been rolled two or three times, yet he still wore his old boots. Charlotte guessed it was because both Pete and Bob's shoes were far too large.

She smiled at Pete and nodded her approval. He shrugged and bristled—making it clear he wanted no praise for his efforts.

Charlotte entered and poured herself the last cup of coffee from the coffeepot. She took a sip of the lukewarm liquid, trying not to interrupt their conversation.

"So where did you live? Where did you grow up?" Sam asked from where he sat perched on the kitchen counter. He was dressed in a flannel shirt similar to Pete's, and she guessed from the grease smudges on the cuffs that whatever he'd been up to lately was something mechanical. She'd know grease stains anywhere.

"I worked on farms my whole life—since I was a kid. Started in Georgia and hopped, skipped, and jumped around from there. Although I haven't been healthy enough to do that type of work in the last few years." Jefferson nodded as he spoke, as if agreeing with his own story.

"Didn't you ever want to have your own house? Somewhere to stay forever?" Emily asked.

"I liked many places. There are nice communities out there. But trying to earn enough at one time and settle down has never been an option."

"Did you travel on trains?" Christopher's eyes were wide, as if he was picturing the man before him jumping onto empty train cars.

"Yup. I hit the rails. My friends became my family, and we took care of each other. I got to know some of their families too."

"They had families?" Christopher asked, scratching his head.

"Everyone does, son. I remember lots of families." A

twinkle brightened Jefferson's eyes. "Everyone comes from somewhere, you know . . . and no matter where you go, you still carry a part of that place—of those people—with you." Charlotte saw Emily and Sam nod, as if Jefferson's words struck a chord with them.

"Yes, these kids here have quite a story of their own recent journey," Charlotte risked butting in. "But they're really starting to find their fit in Bedford." She reached and placed a hand on Jefferson's shoulder. "I have no doubt you'll find your fit too."

"We moved from San Diego just this year," Christopher blurted out.

"Really? I spent one summer in Coronado. Do they still do the community concerts at Spreckels Park on Sundays? Those were the best. Young or old, rich or poor, it didn't matter. Everyone enjoyed the music together."

Sam's eyes widened. "Yeah, my mo—" His face fell. "Yes, we've been there before." He turned to Emily.

Jefferson offered Charlotte an awkward smile and twisted his dirty cap in his hands, as if unsure what to say or do. Pete just lowered his head, tapping the toe of his boot on the linoleum.

Charlotte set her coffee cup on the counter and clapped her hands together as if trying to snap them back to the cheerful group they'd been only moments before. "Who's hungry? How about hash browns and eggs? Oh, and I am hungry for pancakes with sausage. How does that sound for everyone? It's a late breakfast, I know. But I think I have all the fixings." She hurried to the fridge. "I can set an extra plate on the table if you'd like to join us, Mr. Jefferson," she called over her shoulder.

"Well, thank you very much," Jefferson mumbled. Charlotte made breakfast as quickly as she could and the scents brought Bob back inside from wherever he'd been.

The whole family pitched in, setting the table, placing the food in the center, chatting cheerfully as if they were the Waltons in Technicolor. In record time, breakfast was on the table.

As they gathered around, Charlotte motioned to the open chair. "Jefferson, you can have that chair right next to Christopher, the little guy."

"Thank you, Mrs. Stevenson." He sat and scooted in, looking around to see if he was doing it right.

The older man watched as everyone filled their plates. Seeing his reluctance, Bob took Jefferson's plate and filled it with hash browns, eggs, three pancakes, and two sausage links. Then Bob handed it back with a nod and a smile.

"Emily, how many sausages would you like today?" Pete asked, reaching the tongs and a sausage link toward her.

"Ha ha, very funny. The day I eat *that* is the day you put on a dress and head to the feed store." She smirked at her uncle and stuck out her tongue. Pete stuck out his tongue in return.

"Okay, you two. Enough of that. It's time to say grace." Bob folded his hands. Jefferson put down his fork that was halfway to his lips. Then he sheepishly lowered his head. Bob said grace, and when he was finished he lifted a forkful of pancake, then paused, looking to Jefferson.

"I've already called Pastor Evans and asked him if we could have a few minutes after church tomorrow to talk with him. There might be some more work around here that he knows of for you. Maybe even a place to stay."

Jefferson finished chewing a large bite of pancake and then looked to Bob with tears rimming his eyes.

"I—I don't know what to say. I can't tell you the last time I've been given so much. A warm place to stay out of the elements. Two fine meals. These new duds. And now . . . well, it's been years since I've stepped foot inside a church."

"So you used to attend church?" Charlotte asked, pouring a thick layer of sugar-free syrup over her pancakes. She'd bought it for Bob and ate it with him so he wouldn't feel left out, but she had to use twice as much to make it taste halfway decent. Her actions weren't missed by Bob. He grinned at her and added more sugar-free syrup to his plate too.

"As a young boy," Jefferson continued. "My mother, bless her soul, had the prettiest voice when she sang the old hymns." His voice cracked.

Charlotte noticed that at the mention of Jefferson's mother the three children stilled. She looked at Christopher and noticed his lower lip also trembled.

"We lost our mother this year." Emily's words caused Charlotte's attention to turn her direction. "She used to have a pretty voice. But at least we have family—and had someplace to go."

Emily's gaze met Charlotte's eyes, and she smiled. Charlotte felt her heart expand and grow hot with thanksgiving. She took another bite of her pancake, the sweetness filling her mouth, the sweetness spreading through her soul.

Chapter Thirty

Saturday seemed to fly by, especially since Charlotte had slept half of it away. As everyone did their own thing, Charlotte was amazed how easily Jefferson fit in, and she chuckled at her belief that she had so much to offer the man—that she was the one who would lend him a helping hand. Instead, she found it the other way around.

Jefferson, she decided, never sat still. And if he did it wasn't for long. With his help, the rest of the vegetables from the garden got in, Toby's doghouse got reshingled, and he even showed Pete how to use blankets to capture the bats without hurting them. Then, with Jefferson holding the blanket, they'd driven them far from the farm and set them free in an abandoned old barn, much to Emily's approval.

Later, Jefferson helped Pete with that "something" in the barn that Charlotte was now not able to see until he and Sam were done with it.

It seemed as if they'd just finished their late breakfast when they were already gathering around the table again for an early dinner. She'd decided to go all out and made fried chicken, baked potatoes, and a large green salad for Emily. Everyone enjoyed the meal, and when they were finished Jefferson seemed pleased when Bob pulled out the *Children's Story Bible.*

"We read a story every night after dinner. It's a pretty exciting book," Christopher explained.

"I hope you don't mind," Bob commented to Jefferson, sliding on his reading glasses.

"I don't mind at all. In fact, can I ask a favor?" Bob lowered his glasses slightly and peered over the rims, focusing on Jefferson.

"After your normal Bible story do you think you can read the story of creation?" Jefferson didn't give an explanation, and Bob didn't ask for one. Instead he just nodded his answer.

"Well, I don't see why we don't read that story instead." Bob glanced from person to person as if getting everyone's approval. He then flipped to the first chapter of his Bible.

"In the beginning, God created the heavens and the earth," Bob began. As he continued to read, Jefferson's smile grew wider. Bob read through the first and second chapter in his Bible, and when he finished Jefferson scooted back from his chair, rose, and shook Bob's hand.

"Thank you. Genesis has always been my favorite book of the Bible."

"Why?" Christopher asked.

"You know, I've traveled many places, but one thing I took with me wherever I went was my belief in a Creator," Jefferson said, sitting back down in his chair. "In fact, the more I traveled, the more I believed. There is too much variety, too much beauty. I saw it with my own eyes. It all can't come from nothing."

"I've spent my whole life on the farm," Bob said. "I feel the same way when I work."

JEFFERSON SLEPT IN THE BARN a second night, despite the fact that Bob offered the couch. The next morning, Jefferson sang old gospel hymns as he milked the cows and carried the pail filled with frothy milk into the house.

Now, dressed and ready to go to church, the family finished eating in a peaceful quiet, then they all put their dishes in the sink and gathered their things for church. Charlotte wanted to pinch herself as she noticed Pete was again joining them. Dressed in his Sunday best, Pete climbed into Lazarus and rumbled off without a word.

Jefferson followed along as they climbed into the old truck. His cheeks were flushed with enthusiasm, as if this was the most exciting event of the year.

"Have you spent much time in Nebraska?" Sam asked as everyone buckled seat belts.

"No. Can't say I have. I think I was on a train that went through this state once or twice. Mostly I stuck to the southern states where the weather was warmer on cold nights."

"Did you know that Abraham Lincoln signed the Homestead Act that gave settlers free land if they settled here? That's how our family came to live on Heather Creek Farm." Sam tossed his hair.

"People around here used to live in houses made of dirt and grass!" Christopher exclaimed.

"Soddies," Emily corrected. "And Grandma says they were pretty good houses, considering."

"I never knew that about Nebraska, but I'm here all the same, and I think it's for a reason."

"A reason?" Christopher asked. He was sitting in the far back seat next to Sam, his full attention on their new friend. Charlotte even noticed that Chewbacca had been left behind.

"I think the reason might have been to get me to church today. To remind me what matters—*who* matters."

Charlotte didn't know if by the who that Jefferson meant family or God. Either way, she had the same feeling that he'd also been sent to them for the same reason.

When they piled out into the church parking lot, a few of the other families cast them curious looks. When Hannah approached to welcome them, Charlotte pulled her to the side. "I'm sorry I haven't called in the last few days. Something came up. Or rather, someone."

"Another lost relative?" Hannah eyed Jefferson curiously as he walked alongside Pete, striding up to their familiar pew.

"Not quite, although if my family has anything to do with it, that just might be the case."

Hannah's brow furrowed. "I'm not following your storyline."

"Remember the stolen vegetables and eggs?"

"Did you catch the thief?" Hannah grasped Charlotte's arms.

"Yes, no. Not quite . . ." Charlotte was about to launch into the story when Bob approached and placed a hand on her shoulder.

"Church is about to start."

"I'll fill you in after church." Charlotte patted Hannah's shoulder.

She and Bob found their seats next to the rest of the family, and after a quick welcome, the worship leader began with an upbeat contemporary praise song. Charlotte couldn't help but notice that Pete was sitting only one person away from Dana Simons. Yet neither acknowledged each other but just looked straight ahead.

She couldn't help but smile as she sang. The kids clapped along, but Bob stood next to Charlotte with his hands in his pockets, still unsure after all these years of how to follow along to the more fast-paced songs.

When the song finished, Pastor Evans encouraged everyone to greet his or her neighbor with a handshake. Charlotte had hardly turned around to greet Melody and Ashley sitting behind them, when Melody swept her up in a warm hug.

"Ashley told me about your visitor. I think that's just so wonderful how you're helping out. I talked with a few of the other ladies, and we're putting together a clothing drive. Some of them have husbands or sons Mr. Jefferson's size and they said they can find a thing or two. And here . . ." Melody slid something into Charlotte's hand. Glancing down, she noticed it was a fifty-dollar bill.

"It's not much, but maybe enough for a good pair of shoes," Melody hurriedly said, turning to greet one of the older ladies sitting next to her. Then she turned back to Charlotte. "Or maybe enough for a warm winter coat."

"Why . . . I don't know what to say." Charlotte tucked the money into her slacks pocket. "I'm sure it will be put to good use. Are you sure?"

Melody shrugged. "I've been helped by others during a time of need. Feels good to do the same."

The music started again.

The chords to "Great Is Thy Faithfulness" began. And as Charlotte sang she closed her eyes and sang the words as a prayer.

As the third stanza began, Charlotte glanced over at Jefferson, noting that his deep voice trembled slightly as he sang, and she wondered how many springtimes and harvests he'd spent alone, with no one to care for or no one to care for him in return. He sang from his heart.

She had a feeling tomorrow would be a new morning for him, just as today was. A new day. New mercies. And not only for him, but for them all.

Chapter
Thirty-One

By the time Charlotte found Hannah after church, she didn't need to explain who the mysterious stranger was. It seems one of the young teen girls helping in the nursery had filled Hannah in. After all, the girl had heard it from one of the deacons, who'd heard it from the pastor, who'd heard it from Bob Stevenson himself.

Hannah hustled away with a declaration of overcooked pot roast in the oven, and Charlotte watched as Dana Simons also exited the church's front door, giving Pete a parting glance. Their eyes met, and then Pete quickly looked away, but not before Charlotte noticed the slight curl of his smiling lips.

She saw Jefferson standing by the door, and went over to him just as Pastor Evans approached. "So, Mr. Jefferson, how do you do?" The pastor flashed his boyish grin.

"Just Jefferson. I'm doing better than I have in many years, minister, thanks to these fine folks."

A couple of the deacons neared, standing close enough to overhear the conversation, but not close enough to feel as if they were butting in.

"Bob here tells me that you might be interested in staying on for a while if you find the right situation," Pastor Evans said, crossing his arms over his chest.

"Yes. That's correct."

"Well, there's someone I'd like to introduce you to."

Pastor Evans motioned to an older gentleman sitting on a back pew. As if in slow motion, the man rose. His round body moved slowly, awkwardly. His eyes were bright and a large smile spread across his face.

"Jefferson, this is Paul Hubbard. Mr. Hubbard has been a member of our congregation for thirty years. Recently he has been in ill health."

Mr. Hubbard stretched out his hand and Jefferson shook it. Charlotte had seen the man nearly every Sunday, and she knew him to be a quiet and kind soul whose wife had died quite a number of years ago. He was short and round with a red nose and equally red cheeks—the perfect person to play Santa if they were ever in need of one.

"Nice to meet you." Mr. Hubbard bobbed his head.

Pastor Evans patted the man's shoulder. "Mr. Hubbard has a small farm—just a few acres on the edge of town. He can't get out much and he approached me just last week wanting to know if I knew someone who could help with some of the chores. The problem was..." Pastor Evans paused, and Charlotte noted a twinkle in his eyes. "He doesn't have any money to pay for help, but he does have an extra room at his house."

"Are you offering what I think you're offering?" Jefferson ran a hand down his clean-shaven face.

"It ain't nothing fancy." Mr. Hubbard leaned heavily on his cane. "But it has a bed and a dresser, and it's warm in the winter. And maybe you can post a flyer at the feed store—you know, for side jobs, for spending money."

"Now, I suggested to Mr. Hubbard that you both try things out on a temporary basis," the pastor continued. "Then after a month or so the situation can be reevaluated. If either of you has a problem, then either can forfeit the arrangement."

Jefferson nodded once and then lowered his head. For a moment Charlotte thought he didn't understand what was being offered, until she saw his shoulders tremble. Jefferson took in a deep breath. "I don't know what to say."

Pastor Evans shrugged. "You know, we serve an amazing God. Personally I'm surprised by how often things like this surprise us. That's the way our God works." His smile brightened.

Jefferson grinned and nodded.

Chapter
Thirty-Two

H annah's coming down the drive." Bob's voice interrupted her embroidery after lunch. He had opened his eyes just long enough to peek out the window and then he closed them again, preparing to continue his Sunday nap.

"Oh good. I was hoping we could go for a walk today," she said, putting aside her embroidery. She went into the bedroom to get her walking shoes.

A few moments later, the door opened and Hannah's quickened footsteps approached.

"Hello!" Hannah called. Charlotte carried her shoes into the kitchen and found Hannah opening the refrigerator door.

"I'm going to put this fruit salad in here. I made it for dinner last night and went a little crazy with my new melon-ball gizmo. Want to walk?"

Charlotte smiled. "Be back in about forty-five minutes," she called to Bob. "The kids are around the farm somewhere—probably in the barn watching Sam and Pete."

"Okay," Bob mumbled. "But how come I have a feeling they could be making better use of their time? Sam especially.

He could spend a little more time on school and a little less time tinkering with Pete."

Charlotte nodded but she didn't answer as she put on her walking shoes. Within five minutes she and Hannah were walking full stride down the country road.

"So how are things really going? How are the kids?" Hannah's voice carried in the wind. "From the murmurs I've heard around church, things have been pretty exciting."

"To say the least."

"Do tell," Hannah said, taking a long drink from her water bottle.

It was all Charlotte needed to launch in about the missing vegetables, the various entrapments, and their "catching" of Jefferson during Emily's final stakeout. She also filled Hannah in on Pete and Bob's continuing power struggle and Christopher's latest find of the wooden cross, and Sam's continued slacking.

"So much going on. You've had quite the adventure lately. It reminds me of that time when Mike and Carol told the kids they were going to get a surprise." Hannah's words were slightly breathless as her mouth jabbered on as fast as her feet propelled her. "The kids and Alice had no clue as to what Mike and Carol had in store for them. Do you remember that?"

"Are you talking about *The Brady Bunch*? I can't say I've watched that in years."

"Yes. But surely you remember the episode. You know, the one when Mike and Carol come home one day and the surprise is revealed that the Bradys had bought a camper and were planning a trip to the Grand Canyon. Then, when they're on their way, the family stops in an old ghost town and an old prospector locks them in a jail cell and steals their car. In fact, I think that ghost town was actually the set of *Bonanza*. I saw it on one of those TV trivia shows."

"And just what does this have to do with us?" A flock of honking geese flew overhead, their moving V pointing south.

Hannah glanced at her as if it should be obvious. "Well, Charlotte, sometimes we try to guess what God has in store for us. Usually, it's something bigger and more amazing than we ever dreamed."

"But the Bradys got locked up. Their car got taken. That doesn't sound too amazing to me." Charlotte brushed her sweaty bangs back from her face.

"Well, in that episode, yes, but don't you remember what happened next?"

"Is that the episode where Jan got glasses?" Charlotte chuckled. Hannah looked at her in disbelief until she realized Charlotte was joking. Then she gave a polite chuckle in return.

"No." Hannah sighed. "After escaping the jail cell, Mike and Peter take off and find the prospector, and they come back with him. The prospector turns out to be a desperate guy with a good heart, and he apologizes for locking them up and stealing their car—sort of like that guy stealing from your garden."

Charlotte wanted to remind Hannah that Jefferson hadn't been the one stealing from them, and he hadn't locked them up, but she knew that it was much better just to let Hannah go.

Crunching gravel sounded behind them and the putter of an old engine increased in volume as it neared. An old green truck rumbled by, and they stepped to the side to let it pass. The elderly man waved, and they waved back. His slow pace and contented smile spoke of his enjoyment of the beautiful fall afternoon.

"Of course, they made it to the Grand Canyon—but it was too bad that Bobby and Cindy got lost in the canyon while chasing a boy." Hannah tucked her hands into her faded sweatshirt pockets.

"And your point is—?" Charlotte asked again, chuckling. "This story sounds like it's getting worse, not better."

"Oh, the boy helped them find their camp, and they had a great time. Everything worked out. The point is that sometimes we get so focused on getting to wherever it is we think we're going that we forget that the purpose is so often the journey."

Hannah removed her hand from her pocket and slid her arm through Charlotte's arm, linking them together. Their footsteps matched in pace, and warmth filled Charlotte's chest in thankfulness for her friend.

"It's through the hard times that families pull together," Hannah continued. "It happened with the Bradys, the Waltons, and the Ingalls."

"Just as long as you don't say it happened with the Addams family too." Charlotte laughed again. "Although I think our farm was more shocking to the kids than the Addams mansion would have been. Talk about scary!"

Hannah squeezed Charlotte's arm, laughing. "Well, them too. Hard times remind families of what's important."

"And who's important," Charlotte added.

"But back to the Bradys." Hannah spoke about them as if they were actual friends instead of characters on a television show. "Those two halves of a family came together, and Mike and Carol didn't know what to expect—or how the kids would act. They started out as strangers, but as time passed they learned more and more about each other. They stuck together. And they learned what love for each other was all about."

"You know, Hannah, you always amaze me. Sometimes the things you come up with are really random, but in the end they usually make sense."

Hannah released her arm. "Thank you. I'll take that as a compliment." She glanced back over her shoulder. "Wow, we've gone a long way. At least a couple of miles. Think we should turn back?"

Charlotte quickened her pace. "Five more minutes and then we'll turn back, I promise. The farm will be waiting, but as soon as I return, the week will start."

"You say that as if it's a bad thing."

"Not bad, just busy." Charlotte kicked at a rock. "But that is just part of the journey, I suppose. The wonderful, challenging, and always changing journey."

CHARLOTTE'S MIND was so wrapped up in the movement of the embroidery needle in her hand—and her thoughts about what to make for dinner—that she didn't notice Sam had entered the house until she heard her grandson clear his throat.

She glanced up at him, noticing how he tried to hide his excitement under his cool exterior. Yet he wasn't looking at her. His eyes were focused on Bob.

Charlotte placed her embroidery hoop on the table and glanced at Bob, who was flipping through the channels, no doubt trying to find some type of game. Bob didn't even look up.

She turned back to Sam. "It's not time for dinner yet. I thought I had a couple minutes after my walk to get a little handicraft in before I started. Did you need something?"

"I'm not here for food. It's a first, I know," Sam smirked. "Uncle Pete wanted me to come get you. He says he wants to show you and Grandpa somethin'." Sam crossed his arms over his chest. "I told him we should wait to show the finished product, but he gave me a direct order."

Charlotte looked over at Bob again, knowing that even though his eyes were on the television, his mind was focused on Sam's words. "You coming?"

Bob shrugged and turned off the television. "I suppose so. Though I'm sort of afraid of just what this surprise is." Bob pointed to Sam's shirt. "Is that axle grease on your sleeve?"

Sam lifted his arm to get a better look. "Could be."

Bob grunted as he rose and followed Sam outside. Charlotte took a deep breath and joined them.

Sam led them to the tractor shed, weaving through the new tractors near the front, guiding them to the back, where all types of junk had accumulated over the years. Charlotte tilted her head as she noticed a tarp tossed to the side. And there, in all its glory, sat the oldest tractor they had on the farm. It had belonged to Bob's grandfather and it had previously sat on the front lawn as a lawn ornament, until Charlotte begged Bob to take the rusty contraption to the dump.

Obviously it hadn't gone to the dump, but it wasn't rusty any longer. The rust was gone and the tractor shined. It still looked old and worn, but it gleamed—as did the faces of Pete and Sam, who were beside it, standing taller in their joy and pride.

Without a word, Pete handed the keys to Sam. Sam climbed onto the seat, settling in, and stuck the key into the ignition. With a turn of the key, the engine sputtered and then sparked to life.

Charlotte clasped her hands together and looked at Bob. His jaw dropped and he stepped closer, peering at the machine as if trying to decide if it was the same one he'd previously deemed unsalvageable.

Pete motioned to Sam, and he turned off the engine. "It still needs some work, but you should see all the elbow grease Sam's put into it."

"Christopher started it," Sam mumbled. "When he found that carburetor I asked Pete if there were any old machines around here. He showed me this and—"

"And Sam insisted we clean it up," Pete interrupted. "Then once we got started, well, one thing led to another. Jefferson even helped. He said he actually used to farm with tractors this old."

"I never thought that thing could be used for anything but scrap metal," Charlotte confessed. "I thought your grandfather should have hauled it away years ago."

"Scrap metal." Sam's face displayed shock. "Grandma, are you kidding? This is an antique!"

Charlotte laughed, and Bob joined in, still shaking his head.

Pete strode over and handed the keys to Bob. "So, are you interested in helping us fix it? It still needs a lot of work, and a new paint job. But we figured we could do a little at a time and it would be ready for next year's fair. They have that exhibit of old farm machinery that always draws a crowd."

Bob didn't answer. He just slipped the keys in his pocket, turned his cap backward and knelt before the machine. "Sounds like it's running a little lean, but I can fix that. Sam, can you run to fetch a flashlight and my toolbox?"

"Yup." Sam put his hands into his pockets and hurried away.

Charlotte stepped out right behind him, but not before she noted the slight smile on her son's face as he knelt down next to his dad.

Chapter Thirty-Three

After getting two chickens in the oven to bake, Charlotte headed out to find Christopher and Emily. They had gotten better about entertaining themselves on the farm, but they'd never been gone this long before. She'd checked the horses' corrals, the barn, and the creek. Nothing. At least she felt better knowing Toby was with them. Toby, like Lassie, would bring them home. Wouldn't she?

Then, as Charlotte was walking back to the house, she noticed two heads just higher than the dry grass around the oak tree. It was where Christopher had found the carburetor and the cross. Now Emily and Christopher both sat underneath the tree. She placed a hand over her pounding heart and willed herself to be calm. They were together. They were safe.

She got closer and noticed that they were also filthy. Not just average running-around-the-farm filthy, but dusty from head to toe. Each of them had one of her garden spades in hand, and the area around the tree was pockmarked with small holes.

"What in the world are you doing?" Charlotte's question made them jump.

Christopher sprang to his feet. "Looking for treasure."

"Shh—!" Emily gave him a look of disbelief. "Thanks a lot. You just gave it away!"

Charlotte hunkered down, noticing a small pile of rocks and a coin. She lifted it up to look at the date.

"It's 1992," Emily mumbled, "hardly older than me."

"Actually, the thing you need to do is get a metal detector. And if you're looking for treasure you should consider some of the old plots where the soddies used to sit. I read an article once about a lady who found a bag of gold hidden by one of her great-grandfathers. He had buried it under his bed in his soddie and then passed away before he told a soul."

"Do you have a metal detector?" Christopher asked.

"No, but that's a good idea for a Christmas present."

"We have to wait until Christmas?"

"I said it was a good idea, but I didn't say you'd get one for sure." Charlotte rose. "But I like your ingenuity."

"My engine what?" Christopher asked.

Emily wiped her nose, leaving a bigger smudge of dirt than what had been there before. "Grandma just means she thinks we're smart."

"Yes, smart . . . and dirty. You have ten minutes to fill in those holes and then come and clean up for dinner."

"We have to fill them in?" Emily moaned.

"Yes, you do. Around a farm there can't be any surprises. I've seen people twisting their ankles or tractors getting stuck in unknown low spots." Her tone told them there was no arguing.

"Okay," Christopher mumbled.

Charlotte couldn't help but reminisce about the time Bill and Denise had also thought there was hidden gold around the farm. It had taken forever for those bald spots to grow back where the grass had been dug up.

Toby trotted beside Charlotte on the walk back, following her to the tractor shed, where she found Bob alone tinkering with the old tractor's engine. His excitement was evident and he went on and on about all the work Sam and Pete had accomplished.

She watched Bob work and chatted with him for a while, then headed back to the house. Toby followed on her heels.

"Oh, you are a spoiled one, aren't you?" Charlotte said, motioning for the dog to get back outside.

"Spoiled, but cute," Pete said, patting the dog and entering the house with an empty coffee cup in hand. "Just like me."

Charlotte laughed at his joke and then she stopped in her tracks as she entered the dining room and saw Sam at the table with his school books spread before him.

Pete sauntered into the kitchen behind her, set the cup in the sink, and pulled an apple from the large, green bowl on the counter. He eyed Sam.

"Hey, Sam, Christopher is coming to my place to watch *The Empire Strikes Back* after he gets cleaned up. Wanna watch too?"

Ignoring him, Sam scribbled something on the blue-lined

sheet. He read it, then shook his head and erased it. Ten seconds later he wrote something else. Then he erased that too.

"Fine. Don't join us." Pete pointed to the paper. "Keep it up and you're gonna rub a hole in that paper."

"Ha ha, so funny."

Pete took another bite of his apple and chewed it over and over, reminding Charlotte of the way the cows in the pasture chewed their cud. She'd have to pray about that. The boy would have to learn some manners if he was to have a chance with Miss Simons.

"It's a dumb take-home test. The teacher wants us to answer the questions with complete sentences."

"Well, you know how to write a complete sentence, don't you? Noun, verb. Then throw in a few adjectives and adverbs for a little flavor."

"The problem isn't the sentences. It's knowing, or rather not knowing, the answers."

Pete chuckled, then took another bite. "Yeah, that would be a problem," he muttered out of the side of his mouth.

Charlotte cleared her throat. "Pete?"

"What?" He turned to her, eyebrow cocked.

"Don't you think you should chew with your mouth closed?"

He shrugged.

Sam chuckled. "Yeah, Uncle Pete. Chew with your mouth closed."

Pete glanced at Charlotte and frowned. Then he turned back to Sam. "So, does she get onto you like this too?"

"Totally. All the time. I can hardly breathe." Sam put down his pencil and grasped his throat as if he was struggling for breath. After he had received the appropriate laughter from Pete, he picked up his pencil again.

"Does she make you put your dirty clothes in the hamper?"

"Of course."

"And use a cup instead of drinking out of the carton?"

Sam rolled his eyes. "Totally unnecessary."

Pete turned a chair backward and sat facing Sam, tilting his head to get a closer look at his schoolwork and paying special attention to the assignment sheet for his English class.

"Oh and get this." Sam pointed his pencil into the air. "Just a few days ago Grandma *really* got onto me when she found out I was failing in geometry. It's *not* like I'm ever going to use that in real life. Or history, for that matter."

Pete's head flipped up and the smile disappeared from his face. "Are you joking, man?"

Sam slunked down as if just realizing his confession. "Uh, no."

"So you're really failing?"

Sam shrugged.

"Yes or no?" Pete insisted.

"Yes."

"That's totally not cool."

"Yeah, look who's talking. You didn't even graduate."

"Which is exactly why I'm the one you *should* be listening to." Pete's voice deepened with emotion.

"It's not like your life is horrible."

"Not horrible, but, man, if I knew then what I know now I would have tried harder. I put zero effort into my studies and then got mad at my teachers for my grades. I told everyone I'd rather be plowing or milking, and sure it was true at the time, but I can't tell you how many times I'm plowing or milking these days and I wonder how things could have been different."

"Like how?"

"Like maybe I could have gone to college and got some business sense to grow the farm or get my own. Maybe I'd be married and have a few kids by now."

"I didn't know you wanted all that." Sam rested his chin on his hand.

Charlotte felt as if she were a fly on the wall, and she was sure that since Pete's back was to her he had forgotten she was in the room. She stood there, afraid to check the chicken for fear the sound of the oven door opening would interrupt their conversation.

"Well, I didn't know what I wanted back then," Pete continued. "All I knew was that I was tired of sitting in school all day listening to lectures, reading, and having to answer dumb questions I didn't think were applicable. What I didn't realize was that half of school is the learnin'. The other half is the stick-to-it. Anyone can give up and quit. Anyone can walk away, but that cap and gown do more than just prove you've learned your math facts and how to diagram a sentence. It proves you were diligent enough to follow through."

Sam was silent. He sat there, head lowered, tapping his pencil to a slow beat trailing through his mind.

"You can do better than me. It's not too late. If I could, I'd do it differently." Pete rose and turned the chair back around, scooting it in.

Pete turned and glanced over his shoulder into the

kitchen. Charlotte opened the nearest cupboard and started shuffling through the cans, pretending to find something to go with her chicken. It also hid her smile. If there was anyone Sam listened to, it was Pete. She just hoped that he was really listening.

Bob slowly strode through the kitchen, making a beeline to his recliner in the living room. Charlotte glanced at the clock, wondering if it was his book or *Wheel of Fortune* that called him.

"Sure is quiet. Where are the kids?" Bob asked.

"The younger two are washing up. And Sam—"

Before Charlotte had a chance to finish, Bob stopped short as he noticed Sam sitting at the dining room table with his books spread out before him. Bob's head jerked back as if he'd just seen the Easter bunny having lunch with Santa Claus. And then Charlotte thought she noted the slightest smile play on his lips.

"Hey, Grandpa?" Sam glanced up. He ran his hand through his hair. His words and his gaze seemed to be hinting at a question.

"Yeah, you need something?" Bob asked, running his fingers up and down his red suspenders that held up his old jeans. The jeans sat low, under his round tummy.

Sam leaned back in his chair and continued to tap his pencil on the table.

"Yeah, sort of." He bit his lip, and Charlotte wondered if he was going to bring up the subject of getting his driver's license again. Sam had his learner's permit, but they'd gone through the summer with Sam happy to drive once in a while and only occasionally mentioning taking his test for his license. Now Charlotte wondered if it was time for the issue to come up again.

Sam pointed to the paper in front of him. "Grandma showed me that booklet on those cars. And Christopher said something about our great-grandpa and how he helped some people."

"Actually, it was your great-*great* grandpa, and yes, he did. I can tell you the story if you'd like."

Charlotte pulled a head of lettuce out of the refrigerator, pretending she was focused on making a salad instead of being completely alert to the second interesting conversation of the last hour.

"Well, that Dust Bowl thing," Sam continued. "I was thinking that it would be a good story for my report. Grandma said that instead of just having facts it might be good to put something like that in."

"Sure. Good idea. If you have a second, I can walk you out to the spot where Christopher found the carburetor."

Sam rose and tossed his pencil on the table.

"When is your report due?" Bob asked.

"Wednesday."

"Hmm. I wonder if Dana, I mean Miss Simons, would give you a few more days if I ask."

Sam's head jerked back in surprise. "You're gonna ask? What's up with that?"

Bob's gaze met Charlotte's. "You'll see, Sam. You'll see."

Chapter
Thirty-Four

This isn't the way to Harding." Sam squinted out the truck's window.

Charlotte glanced back over her shoulder at Sam. "But there's one stop your grandfather wants to make first. I think you'll like it."

They drove south for about ten minutes in silence. Emily had earphones in her ears and bobbed her head a little to a beat only she could hear. Christopher was absorbed in the game he had brought along. Since it was a special day, Charlotte supposed it wouldn't hurt.

Finally, Bob pulled off on a gravel road, and a minute later their vehicle was rumbling down an even smaller driveway. Charlotte glanced around at the tired farms dotting the landscape, with peeling paint, sagging roofs, and rumble-tumble fences that looked like they couldn't hold in a herd of kittens. Ancient windmills still turned in the gentle breeze, though the law of physics told her they should have crumbled long ago. As she took in the landscape, Charlotte realized that out of all the years she'd lived in this area, she had never been down this road before.

A small house sat at the end of the driveway, and beyond that was a barn that looked as if it had been there for at least a century. The small farm seemed to be only a few acres, and behind it was a larger one with huge metal buildings and fancy farm machinery lined up along the fence. If she guessed right, most of the land of the small farm had been bought up by a corporation.

They drove slowly up to the house, and a short, round man hobbled to the front porch with a cane. The three kids sucked in air, recognizing Mr. Hubbard.

"Is Jefferson here?" Sam asked Charlotte.

"Are we going to see him?" Emily asked, pulling her headphones out. As if in response, Jefferson sauntered around the side of the house with a hammer in his hand. It was only then that Charlotte noticed a ladder leaning against the side of the house and a pallet of bright green shingles on the ground next to the ladder. Glancing to the roof, she noticed the old shingles had been taken off, revealing a black paper material. On top of that, two rows of new shingles had already been tacked down.

Bob turned off the engine and the kids jumped from the backseat. Christopher rushed toward Jefferson and gave him a big hug. The others hung back, taking in Jefferson's short hair, his pair of new overalls, and his bright red-plaid shirt.

"Jefferson, I believe these are your size," Bob said, handing him a cardboard box.

Jefferson's face brightened, and he eagerly opened the box to find new work boots. Without hesitating, he sat on the ground and tried them on. He laced them up, then Bob offered him a hand up.

"Perfect. They fit perfect." Jefferson took a few strides around the yard to prove his point. Mr. Hubbard came to the porch steps and Jefferson strode up to him. Mr. Hubbard nodded his approval at the new shoes.

They hesitated for a few minutes, then Bob cleared his throat. "Well, we can't stay," Bob said, fingering his keys in his pocket. "I'm taking the kids somewhere special."

Jefferson nodded. "Being with those you care for is always special."

Bob just smiled.

EVEN THOUGH IT WAS ONLY an hour away, their trips to Harding always seemed like a fun adventure to Charlotte.

"There's something I want to show you, Sam," Bob said as they left Mr. Hubbard's gravel road behind and pulled onto the paved, rural highway.

"Something for my report?" Sam asked.

Bob glanced at Charlotte and winked. "I think so."

Charlotte thumbed through the many brochures she'd picked up in the rack near the front door of Mel's Place. She always found it strange how many fun things visitors took time to do that hometown folks never got around to checking out. The colorful pamphlets featured information on the Natural History Museum, the Naval Depot, the Super Screen Theater, and the Children's Museum, and she made a mental note to talk to Bob about visiting one of these other spots before the year was through.

Sam leaned forward and peered over the seat. "Are we going to one of those places?"

Charlotte tried to hold in a grin. "Could be."

"Can I see?" Emily asked.

Charlotte pretended to look out the window, but instead angled herself so she could watch the kids in the passenger-side mirror. Emily glanced through the brochures and then passed them to Sam, rolling her eyes with a sigh.

Sam glanced at them. Unimpressed, he tossed them back to Emily, pulled his sweatshirt hood over his head, leaned back against the seat, and closed his eyes as if resigning himself to be completely bored.

Charlotte watched farm after farm pass her window as they drove along. She saw numerous combines in the fields, harvesting. She noticed the beautiful yellow leaves on the green ash trees, cottonwoods along the creek, and silver maples changing into their bold, fall attire.

They passed fields with cows and more cows. Emily moved her sunglasses from the top of her head and plopped them on her nose.

"Wow. We've moved from the California suburbs to a cow-munity," she mumbled.

Laughter burst from Bob's lips, surprising Charlotte. She glanced back at Emily, and Emily lifted her sunglasses from her face. Her eyes were wide—her grandfather's laughter had surprised her too.

"Cow-munity," Bob said. That's a good one."

CHARLOTTE HAD BEEN NERVOUS about what the kids would think of this place, but from the looks on their faces, they seemed pleased. They stood in front of the large fountain, taking in the intricate lighting of the continuously changing jets of water spouting into the air.

"I've never seen anything like it," Emily mumbled.

"And look at all the colors." Christopher pointed. "Green, yellow, orange, red, purple, blue . . . just like a rainbow."

Charlotte looked at the brochure in her hand. "Says here this is the largest fountain between Chicago and Denver. I've driven by it dozens of times and didn't realize that."

Bob sidled up to Sam. "They built the fountain during the Great Depression. It was supposed to be a sign of hope for the town. People would pass by here on their way west during the Dust Bowl, and it cheered them and helped them press on. That's the reason I brought you here—to show you that even in those hard times, there was always hope."

"Wow, does that mean that the people who stopped by the farm—those who lost their baby—could've seen this?" Emily asked.

Bob nodded. "If they drove up this way it's a good possibility."

"It's weird to think of that. That they might have stood where we're standing now," Charlotte said quietly. "They'd been through so much. Maybe this did give them hope for their future."

"Maybe," Bob said.

They found a park bench and sat for a few more minutes, watching the fountain, each lost in his or her own thoughts. Charlotte thought about that family long ago, how much they'd been through. She looked at her own family, marveling at what they'd been through too. Being here, looking at this fountain, gave her a bit of hope as well.

Bob rose. "Ready to go get some ice cream and then a movie before heading back to Heather Creek?"

"A movie? Really?" Sam jumped up, his face brightening.

"A movie?" Emily echoed.

"You mean we're not going to a museum?" Christopher asked.

Charlotte placed her arm around Christopher's shoulders. "You've experienced plenty of history lately without a museum. And I'm not just talking about your grandmother's creaky bones."

"Nebraska history," Sam added.

"The history of my family," Bob said.

"No, Grandpa, you got that wrong," Emily said, nodding. "It's the history of *our* family."

About the Author

Tricia Goyer is a wife, homeschooling mom, speaker, podcast host, and *USA Today* bestselling author of over 80 books. Tricia writes in numerous genres including fiction, parenting, marriage, and books for children and teens. She loves to mentor writers through WriteThatBook.Club. Married to John and mom of ten children, Tricia truly believes teaching and guiding her children daily is her greatest work. Tricia lives near Little Rock, Arkansas and you can discover more about her at TriciaGoyer.com

A Note from the Editors

We hope you enjoyed another exciting volume in the Home to Heather Creek series, published by Guideposts. Forover seventy-five years, Guideposts, a nonprofit organization, hasbeen driven by a vision of a world filled with hope. We aspire to be the voice of a trusted friend, a friend who makes you feel more hopeful and connected.

By making a purchase from Guideposts, you join our community in touching millions of lives, inspiring them to believe that all things are possible through faith, hope, and prayer. Your continued support allows us to provide uplifting resources to those in need.

Whether through our online communities, websites, apps, or publications, we strive to inspire our audiences, bring them together, and comfort, uplift, entertain, and guide them.

To learn more, please go to guideposts.org.